Phyllis Wyatt was born in 1922 in Edithmead, a small hamlet in Somerset near Burnham-on-Sea. Her father was a farm labourer, and *A Somerset Childhood* is the account of a poor but happy childhood spent roaming the lush dairy pastures that border the Somerset Levels. She left school at fourteen, and served with the Woman's Land Army during the Second World War. Phyllis married in 1945 and has one son. After spending many years in Weston-super-Mare, she now lives in the village of Coxley, near Wells. *A Somerset Childhood* is her first book.

A SOMERSET CHILDHOOD

PHYLLIS WYATT

THE DOVECOTE PRESS

First published in 1989 by The Dovecote Press Ltd
Stanbridge, Wimborne, Dorset, BH21 4JD

ISBN 0 946159 72 6

Photoset by Character Graphics, Taunton, Somerset
Printed and bound by Biddles Ltd
Guildford and King's Lynn

Contents

I

The Old House

The house in which I was born and spent my childhood was in the little Somerset hamlet of Edithmead. The nearest town, Burnham-on-Sea, was about two miles away across open fields. In the winter, when the wind blew from the west, it bore with it the salt tang of the Bristol Channel. Tall elms rose from the hedges, and the distant Quantock Hills were framed by the apple trees at the bottom of the orchard. Dairy cattle grazed the green slopes of Brent Knoll, the isolated hill that stood to our east. Inland lay the Levels, whilst from my bedroom window I could glimpse the limestone ridge of the Mendip Hills near Cheddar Gorge.

Few children could have been so spoilt for landscape. Yet there the luxury ended. The family home was a tied house belonging to the farm where my father and grandfather before him both worked. It was built of a soft mellow brick with a pantile roof, and at one time had belonged to a doctor. The half of the building in which Gran lived had a taller roof than our part and the date 1779 was engraved on a stone set above the front door. The half in which we lived was much older. Gran said a butcher had lived there many years ago and our part had been the slaughterhouse. This probably accounted for the hollow ring given off by the flagstones in the kitchen, under which a drain had run. The beams of our kitchen ceiling were plastered over with copies of *The Lancet*. Used, no doubt to keep out the draughts which blew most cruelly in the winter. Years of whitewashing had obliterated most of the print, but when flaking lime was picked off by our childish fingers, case histories came to light and could be easily read by standing on the kitchen table. This activity was much frowned upon by Mother.

Grandmother and Grandfather had come to live in their part of the house soon after they were married. My father and aunt were born at the turn of the century in the bedroom above the jasmine and honeysuckle which smothered the front wall of the house. In turn, Father brought Mother, as a bride, to live in the other half of the house. It was here my four sisters and myself were born. I was the eldest.

Grandfather died when I was quite small. Kind, gentle Grandfather who called me 'his little maid' and fed me bacon rinds as I stood peering over the edge of Gran's breakfast table like a young fledgling, with mouth open wide. Grandfather was a quiet man, with dark brown eyes and a thick bristly moustache. He had a solid silver pocket watch and chain which he wore on highdays and holidays. As well as working on the farm, he earnt a little extra money by catching moles and curing their skins, selling the pelts to a furrier for 4 pence each, which was a good price. An old wooden door with up to 4 dozen skins, neatly pegged out and covered in wood ash to cure them, could always be found somewhere around drying in the sunshine.

I, too, was convinced I could catch moles with an old condiment set container – I was not allowed to touch the vicious mole traps – and placing this in the ground below Gran's kitchen window, went to bed optimistically. I was not to be disappointed. Next morning, neatly entwined in the wire, was a huge glossy black mole. Grandfather expressed great surprise and congratulated me, with a knowing wink to Gran.

Grandfather suffered great pain from varicose veins as he grew older. He was unable to work by the time he reached his fifties. His nerves had given way, so it was said. When the pain became too much to bear he tried to commit suicide. He walked past me on the garden path where I played with my dolls.

'Where have you been, Grampy?', I asked, wondering at his dishevelled state, for I could see his clothes were wet and covered in green ditch weed.

'Falled in ditch', he replied as he made his way indoors.

It was many years before I knew he had tried to drown himself – but the water had not been deep enough.

He once visited Bampton Fair, which had been a rare treat for him. He did not forget his 'little maid' and brought me home a child's wooden wheelbarrow, which I treasured above all else.

After his death in an asylum where he had been placed when the pain finally drove him to madness, Grandmother had to work very hard to keep herself independent and out of the dreaded workhouse at Axbridge. She was determined to continue living in her house, in spite of the fact that it was a tied cottage and the two bachelor brothers at the farm came and told her they now required it to house another farmworker. Gran refused to budge.

'Who', she demanded, 'Looked after your poor, dear mother when she lay dying? Prayed by her bedside and laid her out on her deathbed. Answer me that! So you just go ahead and turn me out of my home. It will give you something to do and the village something to talk about'.

That was the end of the matter and Gran continued to live beside us.

After Grandfather's death Gran continued to dig and plant her part of the large garden in front of the house. She grew vegetables to sell in town, and in the adjoining orchard kept hens, selling the eggs to Uncle Jim, Grandfather's brother from Berrow, who called each Friday in his pony cart to collect them. I listened to their chatter as family news was bandied back and forth, Uncle Jim carefully transferring the eggs from Gran's galvanised bucket to his peck basket. Uncle Jim could neither read nor write but could add up figures very quickly in his head. Gran did her calculations on Father's old school slate which she kept in the kitchen window sill. The slate pencil squeaked and set my teeth on edge.

I was very relieved when the egg money was handed over. Gran was saved from the workhouse for another week at least. I knew it was Uncle Jim and that other man who kept her with us, although the other man never came to call. But who *was* Lloyd George?

Grandmother's flowers were her greatest joy. After Sunday evensong in Summer, friends or relations were asked in to view the results of her weekday labours in the garden and to sip her home-made wine in the cool front room which over-looked it.

On Sunday her working dress and coarse sacking apron were exchanged for Sunday best. Gran made most of her own dresses and decorated her hats to match. She was very smart for a countrywoman. Her white hair, drawn back into a neatly plaited bun was secured by hairpins at the nape of her neck. The shorter pieces of hair above her ears she crimped on special occasions with curling tongs framing her weathered face. Her brown eyes were deep set and alert, missing nothing of what went on around her. Although physically small, she feared no one but God and reserved the sharpest edge of her tongue for idlers, liars and gossipers.

Gran had a naturally unassuming manner and could mix with all on equal terms. One of her acquaintances was Lady Fox, who lived in a beautiful old manor house in the neighbouring village of Brent Knoll. Often, when returning from shopping in Burnham-on-Sea, the open topped car driven by her lady companion, stopped at our gate and My Lady would come in and spend an hour looking at Gran's flower and vegetable garden. Mother usually scooped us children up out of the way on such occasions. Once Lady Fox recommended we use Golden Eye Ointment on a stye I had and rub the swelling with a gold wedding ring. I was overwhelmed by so important a person taking an interest in me. I was so tongue-tied I could not answer when she spoke to me, much to Gran's disgust. I was usually told I had more to say than was good for me.

In addition to acting as an emergency midwife and laying out the dead, Grandmother was frequently booked to take over as housekeeper when local well-to-do families needed help with new babies. After giving birth it was usual for mothers to lie-in for two weeks. Such events were organised well in advance as Gran's services were much in demand. When the expected call came, she set off with her case strapped to the carrier of her bicycle, leaving behind a string of instructions as to the care of her garden and poultry. She usually returned in three weeks or a month later, laden with children's outgrown clothing kindly passed on to us by the lady of the house where she had been staying.

Next day the old Singer Sewing Machine dominated the kitchen table, its loose handle clanging musically as Gran stitched and altered her hoard.

'Keep still', she would command as we fidgeted and fretted while she stuck pins in hems and put tucks in bodices.

We dared not say anything to Gran, but vowed to Mother that we were not going to wear the secondhand clothes. But, as usual, we gave in. Clothes acquired by Gran in this way never quite lost their identity and were always known by the name of the donor: Mabel Dunning's blouse, Mary Green's dress, Mrs New's petticoats.

Aunt Nell, Gran's sister who lived in Cardiff, once passed on a coat which was cut down to fit me. At some time it had been doused with a strong perfume which no amount of washing could remove. I was surrounded by an aura of stale scent whenever I wore it. I hated that coat.

The arrival of Great Grandmother to live with Gran rather curtailed her nursing and housekeeping trips for a while. Great Grandmother was a native of Muchelney, near Langport, and came to stay when she was no longer able to look after herself. We called her 'Little Granny' to distinguish her from Gran. She was toothless and shapeless and sat in her rocking chair in the sun with a large white handkerchief knotted at each corner on her head. She wore a white apron over her dark dress, topped with a black and white checked shawl. She was a tough old lady who had worked hard all her life, mostly in the fields. She often remarked that her children had almost been born out of doors. Mother quietly said that this was where they were most likely to have been conceived. She was convinced they all had different fathers.

Little Granny, against advice, insisted on eating any fruit she could forage from the garden or orchard. But there was usually a price to pay. She ate handfuls of green gooseberries which gave her terrible stomach ache. She drank copiously of warm water laced with bicarbonate of soda to relieve the wind, and called anyone who displeased her 'a mommit'. Any enquiry as to her health invoked the same reply of 'fair to middling, thank 'ee'. She had lost the sight of one eye whilst whitewashing many years ago, a spot of lime having splashed up and burnt it.

My aunt Eva, Father's sister, also stayed with Gran when she came home on leave from Taunton hospital where she was a State Registered Nurse. She was a kind person, with a soft voice and gentle manner, almost to the point of being passive. She was very much like Grandfather. She too, had dark eyes and brown hair and a lovely complexion. She was the apple of Gran's eye. There was talk of her getting married to a lighthouse keeper as soon as he was posted to a house with its own living accommodation.

The knowledge of so romantic and unlikely a courtship added to Auntie's appeal, but she was always a joy to be with. She also spoilt us, making us dresses on her treadle sewing machine, from new materials which she allowed us to chose ourselves. Mother often remarked that she would know without seeing or being told when Auntie was home, for the perfume of Dubarry's Golden Morn talcum powder hung on the air when she was around. Further proof was provided by the gold fob watch which she wore on her nurse's uniform, for when staying she left it open on Gran's front room table on top of the red chenille table cloth. Gran and Grandfather had given her the watch when she passed her SRN examination.

It was Auntie who brought the first crystal wireless set to the house. On the few occasions when I was allowed to listen in through the headphones I heard nothing else but a man's voice speaking from a great distance. The wireless remained a mystery to me. It stood – a box with large knobs and a strange bulbous glass dome – in the deep window recess of Gran's front room, rubbing shoulders with the maidenhair fern in the green *jardiniére*. I could conceive of no useful purpose for the long wire stretching from the chimney to the old pear tree. It had two blobs they called insulators, which I secretly likened to huge, bloated brown prunes. Another piece of mysterious wire ran from the back of the set through a hole bored through the window frame and then buried itself in the soil below. Grandmother and Auntie talked knowingly about 'the earth', but the arrival of the wireless meant little to us children. The world continued to be bounded by that other earth – the familiar green slopes of Brent Knoll rising from the fields around the house.

2
Father

Father, although short like his mother, was broad-shouldered and strong. Although normally a mild-tempered man who minded his own business, he had inherited a hint of Gran's quick temper. This was aggravated when he had drunk too much cider. He was quite good-looking in his youth until he lost some of his front teeth, and had the family characteristic of brown eyes and dark hair.

He had been born in the cottage, leaving school at thirteen to work on a farm, and apart from a brief stay in Ireland during the Great War had never been more than twenty miles from the village.

Grandmother often talked about his having been called up for the war, and how she had walked to the railway bridge to watch his train pass under and to wave him a final goodbye. She said she had debated then whether or not to throw herself under the wheels of the next train that passed. However, Father developed pluerisy whilst stationed in Dublin and was sent home on sick leave as the war came to an end.

He was a great reader and read anything and everything that came his way. We seemed to have a never ending supply of *Punch*, *London Illustrated* and *The Tatler* magazines. These came free from the big houses of the well-to-do in the Stodden's Road area of Burnham-on-Sea. Mother would also buy books from local jumble sales. So father was well informed on a variety of subjects and could converse intelligently with the best. He was left handed, 'Clickey' we called it. Having been made to use his right hand at school, his writing was atrocious.

Father's day as a general farm worker began at dawn and ended at dusk. He never had a holiday, and in principle worked 365 days a year throughout his adult life. His only free time was on a Sunday between milkings. In winter this did not amount to much after the cows had been cleaned out, fed and bedded. Their drinking water, too, had to be pumped from the farm well with a hand pump. Dry cows and steers wintering out of doors had also to have hay carried to them. Every day, come rain or shine, he hitched up the farm cart, loaded it with the 17 gallon churns containing the daily milking, and made the quarter of an hour journey to the milk factory at Isleport. Sometimes I went with him, and the rich smell of the milk mingled with that from the hedgerows as we clattered slowly along the lanes. But should a cow calve during the night, Father would be called from his bed to assist. No recompense was given, or expected. It was all part of a farmworker's job.

Father was paid his weekly wage by cheque. He had never been inside a bank in his life, and mother had an arrangement to cash the cheque at the tiny village shop. I have seen her many times on a Friday, champing and impatient to get away to do her shopping at the larger shops in town.

'Has Arthur given you the cheque?', she would ask Father at breakfast time.

'No', would come the reply, 'I think he must have forgotten it's Friday'.

'They've got no idea how the rest of us poor devils live', was Mother's usual retort.

Father would then hurry back to the farm and return with the much needed cheque. I always sensed he hated having to ask for it.

Father was a poacher. His work jacket had large poacher's

pockets in the lining, and many were the dinners he brought home after a seemingly innocent stroll around the fields. His double barrelled shot gun and the old dog Lassie were his only companions on these expeditions. Thanks to Father's skill we never went short of food. Mother's oft repeated warning when eating game was to remind us that 'those who eats most meat, get most shots' – referring, of course to the inevitable pellets from Father's gun.

In season, game of all kinds hung in our larder: hares, rabbits, pigeons, wild duck and occasionally a partridge. Rook pie was another delicacy that appeared on the table, as did lambs' tails after they had been docked in the spring. Drowned mutton often came up on the menu. This was indistinguishable from lamb purchased at the butchers, providing the unfortunate sheep had been fished out of the rhine and bled soon after drowning. I wondered, as I got older, how many of these sheep had been helped into the water by a well placed push. Mother's only comment to that leading question being 'that a wink was as good as a nod to a blind horse'.

For flushing rabbits out of their burrows, Father kept ferrets. We learnt at an early age to give their cage a wide berth, for they had sharp teeth and an offensive smell, especially in summer when Father had not time to clean them out regularly.

'Can't you do something about the ferrets, Henner?' Mother would complain. 'They're attracting blow flies and stink worse than polecats'.

Then Gran would join in.

'Harry', she would say. Gran always called him Harry. 'Those ferrets need seeing to. The stench is enough to start another plague. You want to spend a bit more time on your own affairs and less on giving away cider to every Tom, Dick and Harry who wanders in of an evening, scrounging'.

Gran disliked some of the hangers-on who crowded into Father's outhouse in search of free cider, and was known to barge in and demand if they had homes of their own.

Father returned one evening from poaching and announced that he had lost the ferret in a rabbit warren. Ferrets did sometimes disappear in such a manner and the usual means of retrieving them would be to get a spade and dig them out. However, the farmer whose land contained this particular warren, was always on the look out for poachers and father dared not risk returning. I noticed the empty sack in which father carried the ferret had been thrown on top of the animal's cage, and sensed his concern.

During the night Father was awakened by a scrabbling on the rickety bedside chair. Lighting the candle he was amazed to see the missing ferret, standing on its hind legs, it pink eyes blinking in the sudden light. It had come to look for Father and had tracked him across several fields, through the orchards, under our uneven back door and up the stairs to the bedroom.

Father bought his rabbit wires from a firm in Misterton who specialised in making them. His writing was almost illegible, and how the postman read the address on the envelope containing his annual order we never knew, but the wires would duly arrive and were soon put to use.

The only other time Father put pen to paper was when the annual notice appeared in the local paper for 'Tenders for the Keeching of Rhines'. Our part of Somerset was intersected by ditches and larger drainage channels called rhines which carried the water to the River Brue or River Axe. It was essential that the rhines be kept clear of reeds, and the scrub and bushes on their banks be cut back. Each year Father would put in his tender, written labouriously in ink with a thick 'J' pen nib on Lion Brand notepaper. His price of 4 pence per rope, a lineal measure of 20ft. was the same each year and always accepted. He tendered for the same stretch of rhine each year. This was part of the main waterway which ran to the River Brue at Highbridge and meandered through the fields beyond our orchards. His tools consisted of a long handled staff hook whose curved blade cut the reed roots and made it easier to flick the reeds onto the bank. He also used a long handled bill hook for clearing the banks. His tools were razor sharp and regularly put to the grindstone at the farm, but a coarse whetstone went with him when he set out for the rhine.

During the long winter evenings Father spent much of his time making spars from withies. These would be used when thatching the hayricks. No self respecting animal would eat hay which was 'fowsty', so as soon as the ricks had settled after haymaking the thatchers moved in to top them.

We had ample supplies of withies growing around the garden and orchard perimeters, their roots well established in the many ditches. If left for too many years before being cut to the trunk the growth became thick and unmanageable, and father reckoned those the thickness of a female wrist were a good size for spars. In addition to spars, they made excellent sticks for staking runner beans and the shorter more brashy withies were used for peas.

With a short bill hook Father cut the withies into six foot lengths, carefully trimming off all brash. They were then expertly split down the middle, their ends trimmed to sharp points, bent in two, packed in neat bundles alternatively head to tail like sardines, and tied with brash. They then awaited thatching time. The remainder of the small brash was made into faggots for use as firelighters. They had to be carefully watched when burning for they would suddenly erupt and spit out showers of sparks.

On warm summer evenings Father went rayballing. This was a method of catching the eels with which the pond abounded. Squatting beside Father I would watch him preparing his bait of freshly dug earth worms, which he threaded on to twine with a large darning needle.

The story was often told of how I suddenly came around the corner of the house and saw a man whom I took for Father, sitting on a log threading worms.

'That's right, Henner', I exclaimed, using Mother's pet name for him, 'String 'em up'. I don't know which of us was the most surprised.

After stringing, the worms were formed into a ball and attached to a long withy pole. With this slung over his shoulder and a tin bath on his back, Father and friends would set off for the railway pond. They took up their positions on the bank and it would be only a matter of time before the eels were attracted to the dangling ball of worms, to be flipped clinging into the waiting tub which floated half full of water nearby. Taken home and placed in the shade, they writhed and weaved around each other in an unending dance. When we were ready to eat them, they were taken out, beheaded and skinned. Fried or steamed with parsley sauce they made a tasty meal. Nothing was wasted. The skins, when dried, made excellent tough laces for Father's farm boots.

The tin bath happened to be our Saturday night bath tub, and we complained loudly for weeks afterwards that our bath water smelt of eels.

Another activity undertaken on dark nights was the illegal and cruel sport of birdbatting. But wages were low and father had a family to feed. Armed with two long withy poles and a large net suspended between them, the men would slip silently to the hedges where song birds roosted. Using a lighted candle in an open sided wooden box as a lure, the hedges would be systematically beaten, causing the unsuspecting birds to fly towards the light only to be trapped by the well placed net. Only the larger birds such as thrushes, blackbirds or starlings would be taken, and were then plucked, gutted and roasted.

Mother cooked them under protest. We children would not eat them. Gran voiced her usual strong protest.

'Harry', she would say, 'May God forgive you for your wicked night's work. You will be found out and put into prison one of these days – you mark my words!'

Father and his friends were never caught, but as time rolled by this activity lost its attraction and the net was carefully hidden, to eventually rot in its last resting place behind the tall cider barrels in the outhouse.

3
Mother

A Devonshire dumpling was Mother. She had been born and spent her early childhood at Eggbuckland, near Plymouth. Her voice, even after years of contact with the Somerset dialect, could not conceal the soft Devonshire inflection acquired in her youth.

She had the only pair of blue eyes in the family. Not one of us had inherited them from her. Her abundant light brown hair was inclined to frizziness at the temples and in some lights looked quite auburn. Her chin was considered to be somewhat on the large side, but photographs taken of her in her Land Army days during the 1914/18 war showed an attractive young lady.

Father had met and courted Mother when she came to Somerset as a land girl. All her own family, with the exception of her mother, had emigrated to New Zealand just before the outbreak of war in 1914. Mother trained for her land army work at Sealhayne College in Devon, and worked for a while on Sir Thomas Ackland's estate, helping with the forestry. After coming to Somerset she became a familiar figure in the Berrow and Burnham-on-Sea area, dressed in breeches and smock, driving a pony and cart, and delivering milk from churn to jug to households in town.

I don't think Grandmother had wholly approved of Mother as a wife for her son and tried to dominate and change her. Mother, true to form, ignored Gran's attempts to reform her and treated all her efforts with usual irreverence.

Mother's greatest strength was her sense of humour.

Nothing deterred her for long. Set backs were not allowed to worry her. Her whole attitude to life was summed up in her oft repeated phrase, 'you have just got to pick yourself up and give yourself a shake, and go on again'.

She bore her five daughters within 10 years of being married, losing the third child, Marion, at six weeks old. Whooping cough, caught from my sister Jocelyn and myself, quickly turned to pneumonia, and being pushed in the pram two miles to visit the doctor had proved too much for her. Marion was buried in the churchyard at Burnham, close to Grandfather. When visiting the tiny grave in later years, we often wondered what she would have been like had she lived.

Mother was a hopeless cook and although we never went hungry her method of cooking and dishing up left a lot to be desired. I suppose that trying to cook on a secondhand paraffin oil stove did not help much. There was no electricity or gas supply to Edithmead in those early years. We had not long been provided with a piped water supply.

Mother did occasional work at the farm for a few shillings, helping the housekeeper with the spring cleaning or other annual chores. Mother disliked the work, but it was rather expected of her. Farmworkers and their families were still regarded in some ways as being fuedal serfs. What Mother objected to most strongly was the sixpences and shillings deliberately placed under the rugs and mats by the farmer, to be found by her when she swept and intended to test her honesty.

Having no other means of transport than a bicycle, Mother walked to Burnham-on-Sea most days with the younger children in the pram. We had a remarkable succession of prams, all secondhand, the only criterion being that they must have four good wheels. When a pram started to shed its tyres, or the wheels became loose and no longer roadworthy, it was abandoned in the orchard ditch and another model appeared to take its place. Mother had been known on more than one occasion to travel the two miles from Burnham with one of her hairgrips stuck through the pram's axle in place of a missing cotter pin. She was a resourceful woman, and always seemed to know where a cheap pram could be found for a few shillings or the exchange of garden produce. They came in a variety of styles and colours. We had high Victorian coachbuilt prams with heavy iron handles. Some with big wheels, some with small. Solid square prams, low prams, twin prams and some that tipped over far too easily.

Mother often related the story of how she had taken a pram to collect dry wood which she had spotted close to the roadside. A storm blew up from out of nowhere. Emptying the pram of its load, Mother jumped in, put up the hood and covered herself with the waterproof apron. A passing cyclist was startled to see an adult face peering from under the pram hood. I could just imagine Mother's almost hysterical laughter as the man pedalled away at speed.

Mother was very adept at picking and dressing poultry. We children were fascinated, and liked nothing better than to stand and watch her open up and 'draw' a chicken after it had been plucked. I invariably watched Father or Gran kill poultry for the table. Mother would not kill them. The stench of the entrails did not deter us as we eagerly pressed forward to see what the gizzard contained and how much corn or grass the poor chicken had eaten before its demise. If a hen still in lay was being prepared, we counted the small unformed eggs it contained.

'She would have laid soon', was the usual philosophical comment from Mother.

Mother had some remarkable superstitions. According to her it was unlucky to view the first sighting of the new crescent moon through glass. Sunlight shining through a window straight onto the open fire would put it out, especially when she had just put a match to it and it refused to burn in spite of the handfuls of sugar she threw on it. Sometimes in an emergency she would be tempted to throw paraffin on the reluctant lighting material, but this was too vital a commodity to waste in such a way. Also it made stains on the blackleaded grate and Father would complain about the smell it left behind as we sat around the fire at night. During a thunder storm she drew the curtains to keep the lightning from striking through the window. She covered mirrors and put all steel objects such as knives and scissors away in the drawer, just in case they should attract the lightning.

We were not allowed to bring peacock feathers into the house or any white or pink hawthorn blossoms. This also went for the white blossom of the blackthorn bushes which flowered during the cold spells in March. Mother was of the belief that the warm weather would not arrive until all the blackthorn flowers had gone.

Any day now, Grandmother would be seen to run madly around the garden and Mother would say, "Granny has heard the cuckoo'. To run when one first heard the cuckoo was to bring good luck and the sight of Grandmother huffing her way round the garden in her full length dress was one of our annual delights, and always a cause of much laughter.

When not walking to town pushing a pram, Mother used a bike which we called the 'milk bike' – so named because its wide handlebars could conveniently carry the two milk pails, balanced on either side.

Cycling home one day with her woven rush shopping bag slung on the handlebars laden with groceries, and a gallon can of paraffin clutched in her hand, her knee came into contact with the can which threw her completely off balance and catapulted her straight into the ditch.

I recall solemnly inspecting the poor milk bike as it rested forlornly against the garden hedge where Mother had thrown it. It was covered in green ditch weed, dead reeds entangled the spokes and pedals. Her coat was also thrown on the hedge to dry and gave off an odour of ditch which reminded me of rotting medlars.

One windy morning whilst Mother was taking a younger sister to school on the carrier of the same bike, an unusually strong gust of wind caught them full broadside and deposited them, still upright, into a blackberry hedge. Mother's involuntary cry of 'Whoa' was the only intimation to the rest of us battling ahead on our own little bikes that something was wrong. We rushed back and above the noise of the wind were shouted at by mother to 'stop standing there like two pennorth of God-help-me and pull her out'.

A neighbour passing by in a pony and trap stopped to enquire what had happened.

'Did you get blown in?' he asked.

'No', said Mother, her voice heavy with sarcasm. 'I always get off a bike like that, and had just gone in to get out of the wind'.

That particular stretch of road for years afterwards, was known as 'The Whoa'.

4
Spring

When the strong westerly winds blew across the fields from the Bristol Channel estuary, mingling their salty tang with land smells of spring, we knew that winter would soon be over. The meadow hollows, full to overflowing with recent rains, reflected the blue sky and clouds. In the orchards the new growth of hares parsley bent and waved in the strong gusts. The bleat of new born lambs could be heard from the sheep pastures. Horse drawn putts with their loads of manure to be spread on the fields were driven from the cowhouse heaps. They creaked and bumped across the sodden meadows, their wheels slithering in the muddy gateways.

The rooks wheeled and cawed incessantly above their half built nests in the rookery elms.

The starlings and sparrows had started to build their nests under the eaves of the house and we were awakened each morning by their chattering. Above the sloping ceiling of our bedroom they performed a never ending tap dance. Soon we heard the squawks of the young birds as we lay in our old iron and brass beds.

Generation after generation of birds had built their nests under the old moss covered tiles. Once, when heavy rain seeping through the roof had brought down part of the bedroom ceiling, it also pulled along with it several old bird nests, all teeming with mites and bird fleas. These fell directly on to our bed.

As the evenings became lighter, Father was able to go gardening after tea. The rich loamy smell of the newly turned earth mingled with that of soot and well rotted manure. Bags of soot from chimney sweepings had to be kept until mellowed before being dug into the garden.

Father was a good gardener and grew all our vegetables. He reserved Good Friday for planting his main crop of potatoes. If Easter wasn't too early all the cows had been turned out by then into the fields, which reduced the work and gave him more time to himself.

Good Friday was also the day of the annual pilgrimage to the top of Brent Knoll in the next village. No one knew how this custom had originated, but it was a well established ritual with villagers and townsfolk. It could have been an enactment of Christ's walk to Calvary, and I knew for sure that when we sang the hymn 'There is a Green Hill Far Away' we were singing about the little knoll across the fields.

Leaving Father to his potato planting, we packed a lunch and with Mother joined the groups of children from Burnham making their way past our house, their satchels crammed with food and bottles of lemonade. Many of the children walked the long way around to Brent along the turnpike road. We knew all the short cuts across the fields.

Reaching Brent village we skirted the churchyard and made our winding way to the top of the hill, stopping at each stile for a rest and to pick out the landmarks in the flat countryside below. The rooks cawed in the elms by the church and primroses and violets peeped amongst the wild hares' parsley on the banks. Flocks of wood pigeons flew up from the trees and in the private wood the burly figure of My Lady's gardener could be seen as he kept watch, ready to pounce on any pilgrim whose footsteps erred from the footpath.

Having reached the summit we selected a spot out of the wind to eat our lunch. If we were lucky we picked bunches of primroses on the southern slope of the hill and took them home for Gran to make the Easter Cross to hang above the altar in church, or to put into little pots to decorate the lectern.

Back down the hill, we ran and rolled out of control with Mother shouting unheeded warnings, varying our return route by way of a lane which meandered over the gentler slopes of the Knoll. Past cottages from whose chimneys the wood smoke curled, sweet smelling and blue against a background of dark firs. Past the entrance to the big hall with its impressive stone pillars. Through an avenue of elms and beech, where a little stream kept pace with us as it ran over the pebbles.

Thus we lived our holidays against a backdrop of simple pleasures. There was little money to spare, and anyway in spring we were always busy. Besides the spring cleaning and the gardening there was work to be done in the orchards – pruning and cleaning round the trees. Hen coops had to be dusted down and repaired, ready for the new chicks and their mothers.

Gran dragged protesting broody hens from the nest boxes and sat them on clutches of fertile eggs which she marked with a big inky cross. Any unmarked eggs which found their way into the nest could then be easily noticed and taken out. The broodies sat tight on the nests until the eggs 'pipped' and the chicks emerged. They were then transferred to a coop where the mother hen scratched and clucked at her brood, keeping an eye skywards for marauding crows and magpies.

I had a little speckled bantam of my own and collected her eggs in a round miniature shopping basket which I called my 'banty basket'. I spent a lot of time in the orchard talking to the hens. They made an ideal audience and would listen politely to whatever subject I cared to lecture them on, their heads moving from side to side to catch the gist. Then losing interest they stopped long enough to peck at the bits of Indian corn, before sauntering off through the long orchard grass, catching at falling blossoms as they went.

My aunt was married in May to her lighthouse-keeper and the wedding photos were taken in the orchard with the blossoms still falling. Gran had made new dresses for Jocelyn and me. They were of red checked gingham and we felt very smart. We waited at the front gate with Mother and threw rice at Auntie and our new uncle as they came back from church at Burnham.

We stood to have our photos taken with the wedding group but Uncle's stepmother said she didn't think we should appear in it as we weren't dressed for a wedding. She made an enemy of Mother for life with that remark.

5
Early Childhood

When I was quite small and before my sisters were born, we milked a few cows and rented two fields. Not having enough acreage to make much hay of our own, we had an arrangement with the gangers who cut the grass alongside the railway line, who raked and collected it for us when dry. I was not allowed down on the line whilst this was being done, but watched from the safety of the railway bridge.

The railway line was the main Great Western Railway route from Paddington to Penzance, and when our milking cows were in Pond Ground which was alongside the track I delighted in standing on the wire fence to wait for The Devonian, with its distinctive dark red coaches, puffing its way up country from the Cornish Riviera. A wave and a shout to the driver and fireman won a wave in return.

Pond Ground acquired its name from the two big ponds which had been dug when the railway bridge was built in the early 1840's. Milkmaids and cowslips grew along the water's edge and yellow iris and waterlilies blossomed tantalisingly out of reach. In the shallows tadpoles swarmed and the aroma of crushed water mint mingled with the eely smell of the water.

Growing from the hedge was a red hawthorn tree shaped like a huge umbrella. Here the cows crowded at milking time in search of shade, their tails swishing and flicking at the pestering flies and the sweet milky smell of their bodies and breath mingling with the perfume of the hawthorn blossom. Never had milk tasted so good as on a hot summer's day when it was milked from 'old Nanny Goat', a veteran cow, and still frothing and hot drunk from the can lid which gave it a unique metallic flavour.

The gypsy children from the caravan parked in the lane came and watched us over the gate, ignoring the 'tresspassers will be prosecuted' notice which they daubed with blue mud from the bottom of the ditch. During their stay in the lane, the gypsies made clothes pegs from the withies, which they then hawked from door to door around the villages.

Another temporary occupant of the little lane was Tom Sweet, the driver of the big green steamroller which arrived each summer to roll the surface of the freshly tarred roads. He never let the roller out of his sight and lived alongside it in a green hut on wheels. During the summer evenings after work was done, he sat on the steps of his home whittling withies into realistic flowers, resembling incurved chrysan-themums. One or more of these flowers could always be found in our house, usually stuck in a coronation mug on the top shelf of the overmantel.

Less interesting perhaps, but with a character of its own, was our other rented field named Brent Ground. This lay in the opposite direction to Pond Ground, being halfway bet-ween Edithmead and Brent Knoll. It could be reached by a footpath or a muddy drove. The footpath was the easier way but it skirted a farm patrolled by a fierce dog which barked and showed its teeth when anyone approached. Mother saved bones and titbits for it but could not win its friendship. So we took the alternative route to go milking when the cows were pastured in Brent Ground.

This drove could be very boglike after rain and the deep ruts made by the farm carts and putts were slippery and full of water. Docks and teazels grew in abundance in the lush undergrowth between the tall hedges, and, in their season, pussy willow, hazel catkins and dog rose blossomed. At the entrance to Brent Ground we were tempted by a bush of large, black sloes, but they were bitter and we spat them out.

Adjoining Brent Ground was Peewit Field. At least, that's what we called it because of a colony of Lapwing which nested there each year. In spring we picked the cowslips and looked for their nests, which were cleverly hidden in the dried grass. They were very quick to decoy us away from their eggs and we rarely found them.

We were sorry when Father sold the cows and gave up the fields. Mother found it increasingly difficult, as her family grew in size, to cope with the milking and to get us to and from school. Grandmother was willing to help, but was not always available as she had her own living to earn.

Without cows of our own we now had to get our milk from the farm. We were allowed one pint a day but more had to be paid for. If Father dipped the milk from the churn we had a jug full, otherwise we were given a bare, measured pint.

Being sent to. collect the afternoon pint of milk was one chore of which I never tired. We were not encouraged to roam the farm, and any chance of a legitimate errand was welcomed. With the old white milk jug clutched like a passport, I would march boldly through the iron front gate leading to the farmhouse, passing under the misshapen ash tree whose branches had grown together, making a natural archway.

The flower borders on either side of the long path had a moist, earthy smell and were a blaze of colour all through spring and summer. At the end of the path a large lean-to greenhouse stood against the high garden wall. In it was a grapevine and many pots of indoor plants whose hot perfumed air engulfed me as I passed the open door. I lingered as long as I dared, then leaving the sunshine behind me, I would open the green door in the wall and step into the cool, open-fronted dairy with its whitewashed walls and milk churns. I usually left by the back door as it gave me a chance to seek out the peacock kept by the brothers.

The postman called me Topsy, the baker called me Martha, but this bird really knew my name.

'Pheel, Pheel', it would call repeatedly.

Off I would scurry to put on my hat and coat, for was not this a personal message to me to prepare for the rain which was on its way?

At least, that's what Mother said.

6

Home and School

Auntie and Father had attended the village school in Brent Knoll, walking there each day by way of the footpath across the fields. When the time came for me to follow them it was agreed that I should go to the council infant's school in Princess Street, Burnham. Wherever I went I would have to walk or ride my bicycle, as there was no bus route through the village.

My first day's attendance seemed never ending. After eating my packed lunch at midday I decided it was time I went home. I put on my hat and coat and made my way through the playing children towards the school gate. However, my early departure did not escape the watchful eye of the headmistress, who stopped me, took my outdoor clothes and put me in charge of a girl from my own village.

At the age of seven years we graduated to the 'big school', which was situated on the sea front. As soon as Grace had been said, sandwiches or chips from the fish and chip shop in the High Street were eaten hastily and we made a dash for the beach. If the tide was in we paddled or tight-roped the breakwater boards which ran seawards from the pavilion. During stormy weather the heavy seas moved the sand to leave huge lakes which we channelled or dammed to our heart's content. In summer we mingled with the holiday crowds and watched the sand artists and sandcastle competitions.

Senior girls were sent one day a week to the Technical School to learn cookery and household management. In the technical building we had a classroom at the top which gave excellent views of the mud flats beyond the promenade. This room reeked alternatively each week of boiling washing or leek soup and stew. The boys had their woodwork lessons on the ground floor and the whole building echoed with their banging and hammering.

I became very envious of the ease with which my school friends joined organisations or attended various events. We had nothing at all in our village. No one ventured far after dark. There was nowhere to go. No pub or village hall. If a journey to town was essential, the bike would be got ready and the carbide bicycle lamp primed and lit. Father kept the carbide in a tall orange coloured tin and Gran supervised the filling of the lamp with the carbide chips which emitted a strong odour when in contact with the water drip which turned it to gas.

For somewhere to go in the summer evenings, I joined the Girl Guides who met in the Church Hall at Burnham. After my first couple of attendances Father put his foot down and forbade me to go again.

'Any organisation which keeps young girls out until 9 o'clock then lets them out into the streets can't be up to any good' he announced.

I wondered what Lady Baden-Powell would have made of that remark.

But as much as I enjoyed the new friends and interests of school, I was at my happiest when roaming free through the fields and lanes of our village.

One of our favourite places was the field across the road from our cottage. We called it the 'hump field' because of the circular grass mound in one corner which was surrounded by a moat-like hollow. It was classed as an ancient earthwork but no one knew of its origin or purpose. Constant grazing by cattle and sheep had worn its sides smooth and we loved to roll down its slopes.

Tucked away behind the 'hump field' was a little orchard, very secret and aloof amongst the meadows. To me it was an enchanted place and the home of fairies and elves. The great elms on the perimeter yielded armfuls of dry sticks for kindling. Here grew the largest blackberries and crows croaked huskily with the morning mists in their throats. At night tawny owls shrieked and called to one another in the apple tree branches.

We were always happy when Mother announced she was either going sticking, blackberrying or mushrooming. The blackberries were sold to a man in the village nicknamed 'Diddicoy Joe'. He was a true Romany who with his family had put down roots and was a respected member of our community. Joe, in turn, sold the berries on to a dealer who bought them for dye.

Father would tell us where he had seen mushrooms growing, which we then left until they had grown bigger. The small button mushrooms would soon grow to the size of teaplates and he covered their tell-tale white tops with handfuls of dried grass as camouflage. When we thought they were ready we hurried along to pick them, going early in the morning to forstall the other villagers, for most of them knew where the mushroom rings could be found.

In his travels around the fields, Father would pick handfuls of watercress from the ponds and ditches and bring it home for our tea. This had to be carefully washed, especially in spring, for frogs deposited their spawn on the stalks and leaves.

It was also in the spring that my Aunt Eva and Uncle Elliott came home for a month's holiday to stay with Gran.

My sister and I gave our usual 'Concert' in their honour, rehearsing it for weeks beforehand. The Concert, as we called it, usually consisted of a short play in three acts, written around the available cast: Jocelyn, her friend and myself. Younger sisters were sometimes allowed to take minor roles, but they were most unpredictable and had a way of walking off in the middle of a rehearsal to play with dolls. We also did individual turns of dancing, singing and reciting poems.

We kept a big tin trunk of dressing up clothes and props. A sheet draped over a clothes line did for stage curtains and an old wind-up gramaphone supplied the music. The programmes were painstakingly written out and painted in water colours.

Uncle loved our concerts, for they made a welcome change to his lonely night watches in the lighthouse. Having taken up his usual position on the sofa, which he referred to as the 'chaise loungey', he would laugh in all the wrong places and get severely reprimanded by Auntie for creating a diversion during the performance.

Mother, meanwhile, had found herself a little part-time job in town helping at the childrens' home. The matron asked us to put on our concert to amuse the children. This we did with Mother acting as stage manager. All went well until just before the final curtain, when she forgot to wind the gramaphone. It started to run down, the music getting slower and slower. This proved too much for Mother who could be seen hanging on to the curtains helpless with laughter. I was disgusted. I took our concerts very seriously. But no one else seemed to mind. The children thought it hilarious and asked when were we coming again.

My aunt and Uncle repaid their enjoyment of our concerts by taking me back to the Scillies to stay with them when I was twelve. Gran took me there, to return in about three month's time when Uncle had his next shore leave.

It was my first taste of a larger world. Yet looking back I

can see that my apprehension at leaving home was eased by being amongst people who shared the same sense of community as us. I swam every day and was befriended by a Scillonian girl who had her own rowing boat. Never had I been so carefree, and I vowed to return as I watched the islands disappear over the skyline from the deck of the boat.

Having been away from the village for three months everything looked different. Summer had taken over in my absence. Sisters, Mother and Gran came down the garden path to greet me. A strange dog bounded at their heels and I did not recognise the leggy creature which tried to knock me over – it had been a puppy in a basket when I left.

Mother, as was her usual practice, had swept and tidied the back path – a ritual that always preceded a homecoming. Everything went before her on these occasions and the dust flew in clouds as she vigorously broomed the hard packed earth. I could see the signs of her tidy-up as I walked indoors to where Gran had prepared a tea of fresh boiled eggs, raspberry jam and home-made fruit cake. I then knew I was home again.

Gran had made up a bed for me in her small bedroom. After being away for so long she thought the rough and tumble of being once again with my sisters would come a bit hard. She was probably right, for we fought like wild-cats on occasion and I had already rounded fiercely on one of my sisters who remarked that I had come home talking 'all posh'. It was not so much 'posh' as pure Scillonian.

7
The Mission Church

Every first Sunday in the month the bell of the little Anglican mission church called a handful of parishioners to Holy Communion.

The church had been built in the early 1920's and was a wooden, tin clad building often referred to by outsiders as the tin church. Before then, services had been held in an old railway carriage which had stood in the corner of our garden. Although it had long disappeared, that part of the garden was still called Chapel Ground, and Father found it stony and hard to dig.

Grandfather's brother Fred had been in charge of the project to get the church transported and erected. It was carried on a large flat carriage drawn by trace horses and came a distance of four miles from the village of East Brent where it had been used as an Adult school.

Uncle Fred never really recovered from organising this epic journey. It caused him a nervous breakdown, or so the story goes.

The building was erected in the corner of a field and a small belfry built to house the single bell. It was then consecrated for use as a church and lay-readers cycled out from Burnham to take the services.

Grandmother kept the lawn tidy and planted flowers in the circular bed. Iron railings fenced it in on two sides. Over these railings the cows came and hung their heads during services, slobbering and chewing and watching with intense curiosity.

A churchwarden was appointed to cut the grass and trim the hedge. He also took the collection on Sunday evenings, the leather of his highly polished leggings creaking as he tiptoed up the small aisle carrying the purple silk collecting bag with its embroidered gold cross.

His pocket watch lay open on a chair in front of him during the sermon, and after twenty minutes his hand would be raised to warn the preacher his time was up. I never did know if this was a mutual arrangement between them, or if the churchwarden dictated the length of the sermon.

On Sunday afternoons we went to Sunday School. Ladies cycled out from Burnham to take our lessons and the boys went as far as they dare to play them up. The ages of the village children attending ranged from five to fourteen and we were divided into two classes. After prayers and hymns were over, the two groups parted company, the younger ones squeezing into the small vestry for bible reading. Here we sat on hard wooden church chairs and drew pictures on brown paper with coloured chalks which were kept on a ledge of the window, in a box that smelt of soap.

I was fascinated by the curate's surplice which was hung behind the vestry door, and wondered how so holy a garment could possibly have so many spots of iron mould.

The church bell was supposed to be rung for Sunday School by a responsible adult, but some of the boys took it into their heads to perform this task themselves, much to the indignation of villagers who were trying to have a quiet Sunday nap. Also to the detriment of the wooden belfry which rocked alarmingly from side to side. The churchwarden too had been kept awake by the din and the culprits were eventually sought out and admonished.

We enjoyed Sunday School, but disliked being made to attend Evensong. The Harvest Thanksgiving service being the only exception. Perhaps it was because we helped to decorate the church on Saturday and brought flowers and garden produce from home. We helped rummage in the church cupboard to find the glass pots with their string handles. These were filled with flowers and hung from the oil lamps which were screwed to the wooden panelling as wall lights. The main lighting came from two big brass lamps with white china shades which hung over the aisle, suspended on chains from the roof.

Gran, as always, made a cross of flowers to hang above the altar. Below the little window which faced east, a painted scroll, fixed with drawing pins, spelt out its familiar message of 'Seed Time and Harvest shall not Cease', again reminding us that nature had completed a full circle since the last time we had read it.

We each took our own little contribution to the Sunday School service, walking up one by one to lay it on the altar step. One year, Gran had packed my 'banty' basket with six brown eggs for me to take.

Everyone seemed to give apples or marrows. The apples, piled high, had a way of rolling off the altar step during prayers or in the middle of the sermon, caught no doubt in the draught of the vicar's flying cassock which always seemed to be too long for him. We giggled soundlessly into our prayer-cupped hands and secretly coveted the large bunches of black grapes which hung on either end of the curtain pole at the back of the altar. These had come from the farm, as had honey in the comb from the farm beehives.

It was Grandmother who insisted we went to Evensong. On Sunday mornings we kept well out of her way hoping she might forget to mention it. By tea time, however, we had usually come face to face and the dreaded sentence of 'church tonight, mind' had been pronounced. Rebel as we might, there was nothing we could do but put a brave face on it and sedately walk with Gran the short distance down the road to the service.

She lectured us on the way, telling us to take our hands out of our pockets as it spoilt the hang of our clothes. To loosen our belts as we looked like sacks tied in the middle, and to stand up straight as we were getting round-shouldered. Gran was very smart and upright.

Once a year we assembled in St. Andrew's Parish Church in Burnham for Sunday School prize giving. At most there might be twelve village children to represent our small mission church.

In the unfamiliar setting of the parent church with its stained glass, pews and choirboys, we looked furtively around trying to spot our friends from weekday school. Then we would crane our necks to see the prizes set out on a large table below the pulpit and hoped our prize would not be a bible or prayerbook. We much preferred the story books with their gaily coloured dust jackets, even if the stories did have a slightly moral tone. Medals, too, were given for perfect attendance.

8

Celebrations

With the number of inhabitants amounting to not more than a few hundred, Edithmead could hardly claim to be a village – more of a small hamlet.

Not to be outdone, however, by its bigger neighbours, it did at one time boast of having its own Harvest Home celebrations in the true Somerset style. These took some organising and without a squire or a big landowner in the village to lend prestige and give support, it was a formidable task for the villagers to tackle. Many old feuds had to be forgotten for it to be successfully accomplished.

Grandmother, who had her own very definite ideas as to what and with whom she would be involved, cast aside her prejudices and gave invaluable help in planning the feeding of the many people who came to the Harvest Lunch. The meal traditionally consisted of cold roast beef and ham, potatoes and pickles, all washed down with draught beer and local cider.

I well recall the first Harvest Home I attended. It was held a little way out of the centre of the village in a large field adjoining the turnpike road. Always very interested in competitive sports, running and high jumping in particular, I had been practising many weeks beforehand and felt I was in with a chance to win a prize or two. But I had not reckoned with a couple of rank outsiders in the form of two tall, leggy sisters who swept the board of most of the children's sports prizes. They lived on the extreme edge of the village and we had not considered them as parishioners or indeed rivals.

They took no part in the life of the village, but nevertheless were quite eligible to join in the sports.

The tug-of-war team with Father pulling at the back as anchor man fared no better and lost every pull. We cheered and shouted them on, but even Father's strong hob-nailed boots could not get a grip on the slippery grass which had been worn shiny with so many feet.

Gran did win second prize for her decorated hoop which she had trimmed with ivy leaves and pom-pom dahlias. These wooden hoops, borrowed from the children, were a feature of Harvest Homes, and the ladies of the village vied with each other to find the most colourful flowers and foliage to decorate them. There was quite an outcry this particular day, as the winner, a complete stranger to the village, had submitted a very clever entry using two hoops joined at right angles and had modelled a thatched cottage to nestle at the base. The remainder of the hoop was then decorated in the usual manner. It was evidently the work of a lady whose qualifications in the art of floral display far exceeded those of the village ladies. Not being able to find anything in the rules to disqualify the entry, the judges had no option but to award it first prize.

After judging, the hoops were hung in the main marquee, where, on a rope slung between the two main tent poles, they twisted and twirled in the eddies of air as the festivities hotted up below.

The last Harvest Home to be held in the village was in the year 1930. This was sited in a field named The Copse, bordered on one side by a magnificent line of chestnut trees.

Gran had been busy for days machining crepe paper dresses for Jocelyn and me to wear in the fancy dress parade. Her dress was alternate layers of red and white frills with a poke bonnet to match, mine of orange and yellow petals with an orange headband for my hair.

We did not win a prize, as the judge said we did not represent anything in particular. One of the village girls went as a 'Hooligan'. I did not know what a hooligan was, but gathered from some scathing remarks I overheard that costume and wearer were considered well matched.

During the evening the 'Black Cat Dance Band' played music for dancing in the marquee. I had been allowed to stay and watch for a while. The Charleston held me spellbound. Auntie tried to teach me to foxtrot, but I thought the business of walking backwards to music was quite silly.

The 1935 Silver Jubilee of King George and Queen Mary was the last big event to be organised in the village. This was held in a large wooden building called The Rabbitry. Cow stalls ran along one side of its length, but when these were blocked off with a huge tarpaulin hired for the purpose it did make a kind of makeshift village hall, even if the smell of cows persisted. The cement floor was broomed to clear the accumulated debris of years, the dust rising in suffocating clouds. Cobwebs were cleared from the rafters and hurricane lanterns strategically placed. The windows were washed for the first time in decades. Startled hens disturbed from their nests in the forgotten hay in the forestall, dashed to and fro, and the old horse put out to grass in the orchard, galloped madly around and around, alarmed at this sudden invasion.

Meetings were held, and Father who was on the committee for the event, assumed a new importance as he instructed Mother at dinner time to get out his suit and his 'collar and hames' for when he came home in the evening.

Nearer the day, hams were boiled and large pieces of beef roasted. Tables were borrowed and everyone asked to bring their own chair. Father even lent his beloved wireless so we could have music. There was some talk of it being illegal to use one's private wireless for public entertainment and by the time the aerial had been slung between the apple trees, the knobs twiddled and station adjusted, we all wondered if it was worth the effort anyway.

All the houses and farms displayed flags and bunting. We had a huge Union Jack which had been used by Gran for similar celebrations during the reign of Queen Victoria. This we flew from a long withy pole which Father had fixed in the privet hedge by the gate. A big red banner spanned our front gate with 'God Bless our King and Queen' depicted in bold white lettering. I was very proud of our efforts.

After the lunch sports were held in the adjoining field. An obstacle race was the highlight of the afternoon. The course included crawling under a tarpaulin pegged to the ground and climbing through motor tyres hanging on a rope. Normally I would have enjoyed this immensely, but I did not feel well enough to compete. Having been introduced at lunch to the new delight of Picallili, I had eaten far too much and consequently felt sick. My sister Pauline had cried most of the day with toothache. Mother was fed up with the pair of us and we went home early.

9
The House Next Door

The house next door, described as 'a gentleman's residence' by the estate agents, was up for sale. It had been a source of fascination to me as long as I could remember. Separated from our gardens and orchards by a ten feet high brick wall, there was little of the house or grounds we could see apart from an upstairs back window which overlooked our garden.

Uncle Jim and his family were living there when I was born. He had a horse drawn haulage business in Burnham-on-Sea and was under contract to haul coke from the gasworks and to take rubbish to the town tip for the council. Father had worked for him for a while when he came out of the army, but had given this up to work at the farm when he married mother. This gave him the right to a tied cottage to set up house in.

I always remember a conversation I had many years later with a lady who was trying to establish my connection with Uncle Jim.

'Yes, I remember him', she said, putting on her posh voice. 'He used to drive the garbage cart'.

Having married into money she evidently felt superior to poor beings who had connections with such a lowly occupation, and was trying to make me feel inferior. She was wasting her time. Having been used to such remarks all my childhood they just washed over me. Farm workers and their families were at the bottom of the social ladder, but it did not worry us. We had many a good laugh at the antics and aspirations of those who considered themselves to be our superiors.

Mother, as usual, summed up the situation in one terse sentence.

'She likes to think everyone has forgotten the muck she was brought up in', was her quick retort.

I was rather too young to remember when Uncle Jim and his family lived next door, but have vague recollections of a huge sow which kept popping its nose over a sheet of corrugated iron which blocked off the orchard from the garden path. In fact, the whole garden and lawn smelt very strongly of pig. Eventually, Uncle Jim sold the house and bought a farm in another village.

Just before the new owners moved in, Mother was asked if she would scrub the house for them. I went with her, and spent most of the morning sitting in the wide sill of the tall landing window at the top of the staircase, staring across at our house – which looked very different from that unfamiliar angle.

In the passage by the kitchen door hung a row of bells used to summon the servants. I couldn't understand how they would know which bell to answer, for they looked and sounded the same.

The new occupants were a Methodist minister, his wife and grown up son. They soon organised Bible classes and a choral evening for the villagers, all of which they held in the house.

In spite of its being 'chapel', Mother attended the choir practice – that is when I could be persuaded to go to sleep in time for her to get ready. For she declared that I always seemed to sense when she was in a hurry to get out, and that I stayed deliberately awake to thwart her. At the meetings Mother learnt a selection of new hymns to add to her already extensive repertoire from the Ancient and Modern church hymn-book. Her new favourite, which accompanied the pram rocking and washing up, began with the words 'One door and only one and yet the sides have two . . .' This temporarily took the place of her usual chants until Grandmother was prompted to ask what was wrong with the hymns we sang in church, and went on to say that Mother would be better advised to stay at home and darn some socks. Gran did not approve of 'chapel'.

The minister kept a cow for the house and we knew when it was milking time, for his son who carried out this task kept up a monotonous dirge, singing 'diddle, diddle, diddle' up and down the scale until the last drop of milk had been squeezed from the cow's udder.

The house had always been known by the name of 'Fernbank' a name that commemorated the huge ferns growing by the front gate and around the back entrance.

One day a new name plate appeared on a freshly painted gate, bearing the unfamiliar word 'Kampong'. The name alone aroused the curiosity of the village, for no one knew what it meant. It was obviously foreign, and the source of much speculation as to who might be its owners.

The answers came soon enough, for the new occupants recently returned to retire after years spent working in Malaysia. They had a son who was at College and a daughter who was a nurse. Later, the son joined the Royal Flying Corps and on his leaves struck up a friendship with Father. Although his way of life was different to ours, he soon became a regular visitor and accompanied Father on his poaching expeditions, becoming adept at using a gun and handling ferrets. His parents had evening dinner and kept a maid, but despite such wealth – or perhaps because of it – Gran never really approved of him. She thought he led a 'fast' life, but could fault neither his manners nor upbringing.

One afternoon, carrying Father's gun, he made his way

alone to the estuary to shoot wild duck as they flew in across the salt flats. At dusk he had not returned. His parents grew worried when he did not return for the evening meal, and organised a search of the marshland. It did not take long to find him, lying face downwards, dead in a puddle of water. He had suffered an epilectic fit and drowned in a few inches of water. Father's gun lay by his side where he had fallen, its muzzle buried in the soft mud.

Of course, there was an inquest. We had not been aware of his epilepsy, but had wondered why his flying career had come to an abrupt end. Perhaps Father had known.

Father's gun was eventually returned to him by the police. Both barrels were choked with sludge and it had started to rust. The following Sunday, with oily rag and pull-through, Father made a start to remove the ravages of mud and salt water. He was not an emotional man, but as he stood in the doorway of his outhouse, gun in hand, the tears streamed down his face as he worked. The lad had become as a son to him: the son he never had.

It was still to be a few years before I was able to look around the orchards and gardens of the house. The wall was an unpenetratable barrier between the two properties, especially as there was a ditch at the foot of the wall on our side. We had two small ladders we used for playing but neither was long enough to reach the top of the wall. Also, the ditch was the last resting place of unwanted kittens and we shied clear of the mysterious looking sacks which could be seen floating half submerged in the stagnant water. Nor did it help to climb our apple trees in the hope of getting a look over the wall. The other side seemed to be awash with fruit bushes and plum trees, and the row of withies on our side with their roots in the ditch just added to the screen of foliage.

At the very bottom of Gran's orchard the wall ended in a

large brick-built greenhouse. The greenhouse extended well past our boundary and into the field behind. A brick had once been taken out inside it to insert a ventilator grille, and it was here we kept our cigarettes and matches. My sister Jocelyn's friend lived next door to the village shop on the turnpike road and could, without suspicion, because she had brothers-in-law who smoked, go in any time and buy five woodbines. They cost 2½d and we managed to raise the coppers between us.

One day as we sat in the dry ditch out of sight, smoking our forbidden cigarettes, we hit upon the idea of getting into the next door garden from the field. Here the perimeter wall was much lower and boasted toe and hand holds. Also, the Colonials next door had left. They did not stay long after the tragic death of their son and the house was empty again. What better chance to explore?

Greatly daring, we climbed the wall from the field and cautiously dropped down on the other side. The greenhouse was full of small bunches of green grapes – it was still too early in the summer for them to be ripe. Tall tobacco plants were growing everywhere and in the enclosed warmth gave off a strong perfume. Then, having explored to our satisfaction the various small outbuildings and sheds around the greenhouse, we pushed on into the orchard where the grass had grown lush and tall under the apple trees and fruit bushes. It was almost possible to look over the wall from that side into Gran's orchard as the ground was so much higher, but we thought it wiser to tread quietly in case we were spotted.

We saw the clearing and pens where our recent neighbours had kept their hens, and the big stack of hen manure and straw which had smouldered incessantly like a corporation rubbish tip, making such a 'smeech' we had to close our windows when the wind blew it towards our house. I think

Grandmother had complained to them about it.

Suddenly, quite close to the house, we came upon a small wooden gate almost hidden by two lilac bushes. This led us into the most beautiful rose garden I had ever seen. The perfume was overpowering and roses of every colour and variety had evidently been carefully chosen and lovingly attended. We stood wide-eyed and speechless, and gazed around us. Although we visited the garden many times after that we never quite recaptured the wonderment of our first visit. Mother thought the garden had been planted in memory of the son they lost.

For many months afterwards when singing the 172nd hymn in church or Sunday school, we would wink and nudge each other when it came to the sixth verse which began 'And in the garden secretly . . .'. We would sing that part very loudly with great feeling.

My fourth sister, Pauline, and her friend who lived on the other side of the garden, decided years later that this route over the wall afforded a short cut for them when playing. Taking the same way in as Jocelyn and I had, they boldly walked through the orchard, only to be promptly collared by the new owner of the house and gently but firmly guided out of the front entrance.

We worried on her behalf for days, but I don't think Gran could have been told of that little episode.

10

Visitors

Gran's sister Emily sometimes came to stay. She was an ardent Salvationist and lived in Cardiff. She was round and jolly and reminded me of her Mother, our 'little Granny'. When Grandmother was out of earshot she used rude words and told Mother quite outrageous stories. We liked having Aunt Em to stay for she made us laugh.

Once Gran caused quite a stir in the village by having her niece's two girls to stay for a holiday. They too lived in Cardiff and were the grandchildren of Aunt Nell. Gran's niece had married a foreign seaman, and this had ostracised her as far as Gran was concerned. She had been to visit us several times, but Gran's disapproval of her marriage was all too apparent. We had not seen the husband – he had not been invited to stay – but understood him to be Portuguese.

The elder girl was tall with features like her mother, but her auburn hair was crinkly and stood out from her head like a bush. Aunt Nell smothered it in coconut oil in an attempt to keep it in place.

Her younger sister had long brown ringlets, huge dark eyes and a snub nose. Her lips were thick and pouting and she had a sullen temperament to match. It did not take Father long to decide that the children 'had a touch of the tar brush about them'.

When Gran called her visitors to tea one afternoon the younger child was nowhere to be seen. We knew she could not have gone out of the gate, for we had been playing on the back path all afternoon. She must have slippped off some-

where when Gran had gone upstairs to wash and Aunt Nell
had dozed in the sun. The farmworker on the farm next door
heard us calling and came across to say he had seen a small
child running down the drove which led to the fields behind
our orchards. We clambered over the low wall and ran down
the drive way, shouting the child's name. She was nowhere
to be seen. We ran across the field. Aunt Nell, unused to
such uneven terrain, was soon left well behind, but Gran,
apron strings flying behind her, forged on ahead with Mother
making a close second. They were spurred on, no doubt, by
visions of the missing child floating 'Ophelia-like' in the big
rhine which flowed at the far end of the field.

Before we even saw her, we heard her, shouting and bellow-
ing, with, as Mother so aptly described, 'her mouth as wide
as a turnpike gate'. She was on the far side of the rhine,
having crossed by the footbridge. A feat in itself for a small
child to accomplish. Once over she started to walk across
the next field, only to be confronted by several curious cows
who walked up to her and then stood and stared. Fearful of
being eaten alive she turned back to the bridge, only to find
her nerve had gone and she was unable to re-cross. We never
did find out where she intended to go.

'Poor little soul', said Mother, compassionately, when all
the hullabaloo had died down. 'I hope she never meets up
with anything worse in life than a few innocent cows'.

After Aunt Nell's death several years later, the children
did not visit us again and we lost touch with them.

The most unwelcome visitors to the village, disliked even
more than the gypsies, were the horses, riders and hounds
of the local hunt. They met in the area several times during
the season, galloping across pastures, through hedges and
ditches, and leaving a trail of destruction in their wake. There
was plenty of drowned mutton the week after a meet, and

many aborted calves, as sheep and cows scattered before them. Yearlings escaped through hedges and got mixed up with herds running with a bull with inevitable consequences. The milking cows were uneasy and would not give down their milk at milking time, which then took twice as long as usual.

Father was also annoyed because the hunt upset his poaching activities. Normally he knew where his quarry could be found and could plot their comings and goings. The hunt disturbed the natural rhythms of country life and it took days before he could be certain of not returning home empty-handed. It also meant extra work for the farm hands, for fences were broken and hedges in need of repair.

None of the local farmers were members of the hunt, and hardly any of them rode to hounds. The horses kept on the farms were working horses – hunters were for the gentry. It was advisable, however, to throw open one's land to the chase.

As children we knew nothing of all this and thought 'a meet' to be most exciting. Should the hounds come near the home fields we chased after them and followed on foot, running miles across the countryside. Once the hounds came through our orchard. We ran indoors, fearful for the safety of our pet Angora rabbit which was allowed to roam free under the apple trees. Luckily a blast on the hunting horn called them away before they could scent it.

It was usual to stop for refreshments at midday, the farmers taking it in turns to be host to the hunt. Hunks of bread and cheese were supplied and laid out on trestles in barns or outbuildings. Cider would also be handed around. Having chased the hunt for many miles and coming to rest in a farmyard, my sister and I saw no reason why we should not enjoy some of the refreshments provided. After all we had opened and closed gates for the huntsmen during the day, and had held the reins of a horse when a lady remounted after being thrown.

We were sitting on a log enjoying our bread and cheese when a farm dog came up and snatched the bread from my hand, giving me a nip at the same time. With thoughts of rabies and lockjaw uppermost in my mind, I quickly made my way home to wash and put iodine on the bite, which turned out to be nothing more than a slight scratch.

Mother said it served me right – we had no business to eat the bread and cheese, as it was not provided for the likes of us.

Apart from our relatives and friends, and relatives of neighbours, strangers in the village were looked upon with suspicion. All the tradesmen were well known and accepted without question.

A twice yearly visitor was old Bill with his beautiful stud stallion. His short, square figure, dwarfed by the magnificent animal, was a familiar sight in spring and summer as they tramped side by side from village to village, calling at farms wherever the stallion's services were required.

On these occasions, when in our neighbourhood, the horse was stabled at the farm, whilst Bill spent the night with us, sleeping on the red leather sofa in the front room.

Bill was one of the few people to ever use the front room, for we rarely entered it, even in winter. It was kept for 'best' while we huddled in the kitchen around the old range on a huge curved, wooden settle whose hard seat protected our backs from the whistling draughts.

The only other visitors to the front room were a death-watch beetle which ticked away behind the panelling, and a couple of lizards who lived in the thick wall and occasionally came out and hid behind the sofa. When we eventually used the room in later years and the fire was lit, the lizards disappeared for good.

If such visitors were rare, others were more frequent. The baker from Burnham called every day in his motor van, and the butcher twice a week with his horse and high cart, the meat hanging on metal hooks above the wooden chopping board.

The coalman came on Mondays on a flat four-wheeled wagon. It was drawn by a huge shire horse whose brasses gleamed and whose mane and tail were plaited with red and blue ribbons. Coal was an expensive item, and we rarely could afford more than one hundredweight a week.

The coalman's horse caused us some annoyance in the summer or dry weather, for it had a habit of urinating just outside our gate whilst standing waiting for our coal to be brought in. It was probably its first stop since leaving town, with the result that the area outside the gate soon stank in the hot sunshine. Characteristically, Gran did not let the matter rest, and suggested to the coalman that he gave the horse a chance to do what was necessary before arriving in the actual village.

With tobacco stained teeth clenched around the briar pipe which never left his mouth, back came the reply from the coalman.

'Missus', he said, 'I haven't got time to stop in every gateway between here and Burnham. I suggest you have a word yersel' with t'old hoss, because her won't take any notice of what I tell un'.

So we had no alternative but to take buckets of water to the gateway and swill away the smell of horse.

The warm days of summer also caused our primitive drainage system to smell. The open fronted wash house with its copper, bench and mangle had the only water tap which was shared between Gran's part of the house and ours. It was just a standpipe with no sink and the waste water ran straight into a drainage system of small field pipes which carried it to an open ditch. Here the blue black mud oozed and bubbled and the mosquitos danced above the towering elder bushes which overhung it. Occasionally one of the field pipes would crack and cave in, causing waste water to dam and flood the wash house. This seemed to happen most frequently on wash days and Mother or Grandmother, according to whose wash day it was, sloshed ankle deep in soapy water which refused to drain away.

Each rinsing only aggravated the problem, until the water eventually overflowed into the ashpit beneath the clothes copper, causing the hot ash to sizzle and spit and give off a pungent odour. We children said it smelt like steamrollers.

Tempers were frayed as clothes were pummelled and rubbed in the wooden tub on the bench, then put through the rickety mangle, the legs of which by now would be well awash. The whites, after their boil-up in the copper, were rinsed in a large earthenware pan full to the brim of Reckett's blue water. Then out to the clothes line in the orchard, pegged and propped and left to billow and flap in the breeze which always blew under the apple and walnut trees.

The chimney of the wash house, which was a glazed pipe cemented to a brick base, continued to belch forth smoke among the branches of the lilac tree which had grown around it. The flood in the wash house deepened. Father would be reminded at dinner time to borrow the rods from the farm. These doubled for chimney sweeping or drain clearing. Once Father had located the blockage, he dug down and replaced the broken pipe and we cheered and ran to the ditch to watch the pent-up water appear in a rush, frightening the sparrows and starlings that had been foraging in the ditch.

To me, each house in the village had its own particular smell. I could have guessed which house I was in, even if blindfolded.

A cottage in the lane smelt of warm tea cosies and brown mint humbugs. I was usually given a mint when visiting here with Mother. One farm kitchen was full of coats and rainwear which seemed to exude a perpetual smell of stale frying. Another very old cottage reeked of Monday washday soap-suds every day of the week.

One house which intrigued me was a long, stone built cottage with a slate roof, built close to the turnpike road. It was aptly named Greystones. Its inhabitants, a Mr and Mrs Hughes, kept a huge Chow dog with a blue mouth and tongue. The house was a overnight stop and recognised lodging house for tramps. It smelt of damp and old clothes. She was a short, plump little woman and a staunch Roman Catholic. Her husband, physically her exact opposite, collected rags and bones. He toured the villages to do his totting with a flat-based four-wheeled cart, which he drove from a high iron seat behind the horse.

I dreaded going into the house, should Mother decide to make a call when we were out for a walk, fearfully looking into corners to see if any tramp had been left over and forgotten from the night before.

Another acquaintance of Mother's was a rather dirty old soul with a heart of gold. She always had something to give away, many of the items having been given to her by the ladies or cooks of the big houses where she worked. Anything that was sealed like pots of jam we felt quite safe in eating. Basins of tasty beef dripping were always acceptable providing the seal of fat was unbroken. Anything mother was unsure of was thrown to the hens as soon as we got home.

The old lady had come to the village late in life to marry

one of the local widowers, and many were the jokes played on the old couple after their wedding. No one claimed responsibility for these or the culprits found out, but I know that Father and his friends grinned slyly whenever the incidents were mentioned and guffawed into their cider mugs for weeks afterwards.

11

High Summer

It was now high summer and the flower gardens around the house were a blaze of colour. Thrushes cracked open snails upon the stones of the front path. The sun beat down upon the front door, releasing the scent of more than a hundred summers from the seasoned wood, to mingle with the perfume of stocks and jasmine and to drift into the house on the breeze.

Flies swarmed in the kitchen, and the sticky flypapers were black to overflowing with their trapped bodies.

The meadow grasses had grown thick and tall. We loved to be able to walk home from Burnham by way of the footpath which skirted the mowing fields, picking the white moon daisies and looking for quaking grass which we called 'shackle grass'.

Early each morning the horse drawn mowing machines set out from the farms, their iron wheels leaving an unmistakable criss-cross pattern on the softening tar of the road. Razor sharp blades, newly filed and honed, were clad in sacking for protection which made them resemble flying brown pennants when lifted for transportation.

Haymaking had begun.

Soon the whirr of the machines and the scent of newly cut grass completely dominated the countryside. Row upon row of neatly cut swathes lay drying in the sun, to be turned over by hand raking then tedded by machine until dry and ready to be put into haycocks to await picking up by the wagons.

Once hay hauling had commenced Father would have a

hasty tea and return to the farm where the wooden haycarts stood ready, and the cider jars were kept filled.

No one would dream of working for a farmer who didn't supply cider during the haymaking. Father took his in a gallon stone jar with a loop of haycord tied around the neck. The loop helped to keep the jar steady when he slung it up to his mouth to drink, resting it on the crook of his arm to take the weight.

Anyone who could pitch hay, load a wagon or make a rick were pressed into service. Some farmers preferred to rely on their own workforce, others joined forces and helped each other.

Late into the evening until the dew began to fall the full wagons creaked their way to the outdoor ricks or back to the farmyard hayhouses, jolting through gateways barely wide enough to take the overhanging loads, and leaving trails of hay on hedges and trees.

The heavy shire horses sweated and strained, their harness creaking. Pestered by horse-flies, their flanks quivered at each bite. They did not flinch when we killed off the flies one by one with the flat of our hands.

Everywhere at home there were hayseeds. They lay scattered on the kitchen floor and a trail led up the stairs. They poured from Father's hobnailed boots as he tipped them upside down. His woollen socks bristled. The indentation on the crown of his old working trilby hat was full and they dug and scratched his skin through the thick white and blue striped Oxford shirting of his collarless shirt.

Mother complained loudly and wielded the broom with vigour, making the dust fly from the threadbare carpets and mats, which for some reason she always referred to as 'the Brussels'.

One summer, during the haymaking season, an extra

labourer was taken on at the farm, and Gran was asked to
board him. He was Irish, a Catholic, and answered to the
name of Joe. He was scrupulously clean and washed every
morning and evening in a tub of cold water which Gran
placed for him on the bench outside. He walked to Burnham
to Mass each Sunday. Gran was not particularly keen to feed
him, but it was only for a short while and the money came
in handy. She did feel though that the housekeeper at the
farm could easily have lodged him, for there were ample
empty beds in the farmhouse. One did not, however, question
farm housekeepers. They were an elite band, who by virtue
of their employment were regarded with respect and accorded
a high standing in the community.

For us children haymaking coincided with the long summer
holiday – and that meant the seaside. Leaving a cold meal
for Father, we would set off for the beach at Burnham for
a day's outing, the pram piled high with baby, buckets and
spades, bathing costumes and towels.

It was almost an hour's walk to the sands. As mother could
not bear to be late for anything, we arrived and took up
position before most of the holiday makers were out of bed.

The estuary, which has the second highest ebb and flow
of water in the world, has a tide which was invariably out
miles beyond the mud flats, but we were quite content to
paddle and try to swim in the paddling pool. Mother made
sandcastles and pies for the younger ones and they were quite
happy until the hot sun and sea air took their toll and made
them tired and fractious.

We would be ordered to get dressed, with the added warning that if we stayed in the water any longer we would become
'zammy-soaked'. This was Mother's word for water-logged.
Then dried, dressed and glowing, we were sent on to the
esplanade to find a Walls 'Stop Me and Buy One' tricycle to

Me and my great grandmother, who came from Muchelney and who we
called 'Little Granny'.

Tom and Mary Rice, my grandfather and grandmother on my father's side.

Ada and Harry Rice, my parents, looking typically cheerful.

(above) Me and the chickens.   *(below)* My sister Jocelyn, me and Gran.

All of us with Gran, *(left to right)* Margaret, Jocelyn, me and baby Pauline.

purchase a penny cornet or three-cornered Sno Frute. We were then given another penny so we could sit and watch the beach show for an hour while Mother went to the shops.

The show never shed its lustre, although we knew every act backwards. It was a family show named Freddie Fay's Frolics, which came every year and stayed until the last visitor had gone and the autumn high tides threatened to wash its wooden structure away.

We laughed at Freddie in his cap and plusfours; at the pack of Pekinese dogs belonging to his wife who wound themselves around the piano legs to the point of strangulation as their leads got shorter and shorter. We clapped their daughter, Erin, who tap danced, sang and did amazing back-bend acrobats and splits. There was also a male entertainer who juggled and twirled batons, and two or three girl dancers who tap-danced and high kicked in unison. So happy it hurt, we shouted and cheered from our hard seat on the stones.

Three o'clock found us making our way home, fortified with a bag of sweets.

Mother insisted on being home in time to get Father's tea. Dinner he could cope with. Cold meat or cheese he could manage, but she must be home to get his tea. I never knew him once make a pot of tea or cut a slice of bread and butter.

While the men toiled in the fields, the women folk were also busy around the garden and house. Grandmother had already shrouded the raspberry canes in old lace curtains to keep the birds from ripening fruit. She took orders for raspberries from shops in town and would set off after breakfast with her bicycle basket piled high with laden punnets. The remainder of the raspberries would be made into jam, and for days Gran's kitchen resembled a miniature jam factory, the contents of the shiny maslin pan blending its aroma with the smell of the paraffin stove on which it simmered.

file 59

Gooseberries and blackcurrants were also made into jam, and the smell of fruit pies drifted tantalisingly through Gran's back door.

Soon the small, early pears would begin to fall, to be pecked to pieces by the hens before we could collect them. One branch of the pear tree hung over the garden fence and the fruit, safe from the beaks of the hens, fell into a clump of pink phlox, which dispersed its heady, distinctive perfume as we brushed through searching for the pears.

Our other summer outing was on Bank Holiday Monday when Mother took us to see the carnival procession in aid of the Burnham War Memorial Hospital. It always seemed to rain on Bank Holiday Mondays.

One year, just as the procession had passed, the sky darkened ominously and thunder could be heard rumbling in the distance. Huge spots of rain started to fall and Mother decided to dash for shelter with the pram and younger sisters.

Jocelyn and I said we were going to make a run for it and try and get home before the storm broke. Before we reached it the threatened deluge caught up with us and soaked us to the skin. To make matters worse the dye had run from our navy blue knickers and had coloured our beautiful new white shorts a drab shade of blue which no amount of boiling ever removed.

To add to our troubles we lost Aunt Nell. She was staying with Gran for a holiday and was nowhere to be found when we finally arrived home. She had chosen to stay behind and sit in the garden when we all went to the Carnival.

We eventually found her cowering in Gran's indoor coalhouse with the door firmly shut. She was terrified of thunder and lightning.

On the Wednesday after the Bank Holiday it was the childrens' Carnival with a procession and stalls and amusements in the Manor Gardens. From these stalls we obtained our supply of Tokalon face powder. For a few pence we could buy a box of samples containing sachets of varying shades and it even included green powder for shading. Grandmother usually told us to 'take that muck off your faces' if she caught us using it. Anyway, we thought it better than the custard powder which one of the village girls used when she came to Sunday School.

12

Autumn and Harvest

Father had planted a walnut tree in the orchard when he and Mother were first married. It had grown quickly and was soon big enough to take our swing. Oh! the exhilaration of soaring into the green of its branchs, or carefully climbing to its summit, where birds swayed amidst twigs.

Father had also planted a Beauty of Bath apple tree. It was the first to ripen in late August and we were not allowed to pick any of the fruit until Father had selected the best for his entry in the annual Burnham flower show. Before the birds had a chance to peck them, they were carefully picked and taken indoors to finally ripen on the wide sill of the front room window and attain the rosy hue so much prized for show fruit. On the day of the show they were polished with a silk handkerchief to give them a high gloss. Father usually carried off the prize for Beauty of Bath apples in the Cottager Class.

Vegetables, and sweetpeas were also entered by Father, though he cared particularly about onions, parsnips and carrots.

There was always excitement when the lovely sweetpea vases with their silver bases and long glass stems were carefully taken out of their tissue paper wrappings and polished ready for the show. The row of colourful sweetpeas were inspected daily and a mental note made of long stems with fine blooms.

All the show entries were loaded into the farm cart and taken to the show early in the morning to the big marque for staging. Gran accompanied Father. She supervised the arrangement of the sweetpeas in their vases.

There was a Morgan Sweet apple tree at the bottom of the orchard which had fallen over in a gale. It was, in turn, our ship, tree house or lighthouse and was an easy climb for younger sisters to join in our games.

The two breeding sows, Alice and Dinah, when not suckling piglets in the sty, used the tree as a scratching post and we amicably shared this fenced off part of the orchard with them. Father had started to keep breeding sows after he sold the cows. They proved to be expensive to feed and we were often short of money when the time came to replenish their sacks of barley meal.

One day, Dinah suddenly stopped rooting around, and with her little eyes glinting malevolently made a dash at me. I fled to the half fallen Morgan Sweet and sought refuge in its top branches, whilst she stood below with her fore-feet on the sloping trunk, grunting wickedly. I remembered all the stories I had heard about pigs eating human flesh and shouted to Jocelyn to distract the animal's attention by rattling the feeding bucket. The ruse worked. The sow, always greedy for food, ran off towards the sty. I slid down the tree and fled the intervening distance to the fence which I leapt with one bound.

As soon as the Morgan Sweet apples ripened, so our circle of friends widened. Mother threw out invitations to all and sundry to come and help themselves to fall-downs. On Saturdays they came, armed with the biggest shopping bags they could find. They scroffed and scrumped and finally staggered back to town hardly able to carry the baskets they had filled to overflowing.

I found I was very popular with schoolmates at this time of year. Sometimes we took a barley meal bag full of apples to school and left them at the classroom door for the children to help themselves. One year the headmaster insisted I stood by the bag of apples and that each child should thank me as they took an apple on their way out to the playground. I was so embarrassed I could have cried.

The orchard grass soon disappeared under a carpet of apples. Mother worked hard each day to clear the ground and the cider heap became bigger and bigger until it was necessary to fence it around with wire netting and old railway sleepers. The hens flew in and perched on the top of the heap, pecking at the fruit and leaving their droppings. Father jokingly remarked that it all helped to make a good brew.

Still the ripe fruit fell. We could hear the dull thuds as they landed on the roof of the pig sty or fell on the hard packed earth by the orchard gate. The walnuts too tumbled through the thick leaves of the walnut tree, shedding their green casings as they hit the ground. This pungent smelling outer shell stained hands an ochre colour which even soap and water did not completely remove.

The keeping apples, the Blenheims and Bramleys, were carefully picked and carried indoors and then taken upstairs to the low ceilinged back bedroom or to the loft above the kitchen where they were laid in rows on sheets of newspaper.

Mother gathered up the walnuts in her apron and these were put to dry on the wide front room window sill until they were ready to lay side by side with the apples. In the quiet of the night when the moon shone through the small leaded panes of the low window, the mice popped up from holes in the floorboards and played contentedly, chasing and rolling the nuts across the floor. Soon the upper part of the house smelt of the mellowing fruit, intermingling with the stronger smell of drying onions.

By now, Father had brought out the tall cider barrels from

the outhouse. Each one was carefully washed clean of the dregs of last years cider, which by now tasted like vinegar. They were lined up along the garden path to freshen in the air in readiness for the sniffing test Father would give them. Bungs were replaced and iron hoops coopered into position where necessary. Father was a good cooper. He could also renew the bottom of a peck or bushel basket with fresh withy. He had never been taught, but his grandfather had been a basket maker at Muchelney, so it must have been an inherited skill.

Father took the opportunity when the barrels were taken from the outhouse to give it a good clean. The smelly sacks on which the dog, Lassie, slept were taken out and burnt. Wheelbarrow loads of loose earth were shovelled up from the floor, each load containing a good sprinkling of empty Star cigarette packets. Father smoked Star cigarettes for many years and we carefully collected all the sets of cards. The black cobwebs which hung in strips from the rafters were left undistrubed. The old bicycle frames, hay knives, scythes, mole traps and eel spears which hung on the wall were allowed to gather more rust.

Father made enough cider from our own apples to last him through the year. His old pint cider mug with its broken handle and farmers' prayer inscribed on it was passed around his friends during their evening get-togethers in the outhouse. There in the biting cold of the winter they stood drinking and yarning, the only light coming from the flickering candle stuck with its own grease in an orange box fixed to the wall. This box was filled to overflowing with tins of rusty nails, string, haycord and various tools.

On the top of the box Father kept his rabbit snares and a big brass telescope which he used on Sundays and summer evenings to watch the people walking on Brent Knoll. An old piece of sacking draped across the window kept some of the draught at bay and also concealed the candle light from unwanted passers-by who might otherwise be tempted to call.

After his friends had gone, Father came indoors complaining of the cold and stamping around in his hobnailed boots to get the circulation back to his frozen feet. Mother chided him for being so foolish. Grandmother went even farther and made pointed remarks in the hearing of his friends to the effect that it was a pity that some people didn't have something better to do than to waste time drinking cider.

I had drunk cider for supper as long as I could remember. One year Father had made a very special brew which he reserved for our own use. This was kept in the larder in a small barrel which had previously held rum – consequently the contents were unusually potent. As most wooden taps dripped, a large jam jar was placed beneath to catch the droppings. It soon became full. Having evaded the watchful eye of Mother, I saw no reason why the drippings in the jar could not be drunk and promptly drained it to the last dregs.

Mother found me some while later in a semi-alcoholic stupour, propped against the wall of the larder grinning foolishly. She carried me into the kitchen and sat me on the wooden settle by the fire. I hiccuped and fell to the floor. I was then hurriedly undressed and put to bed to sleep it off before Grandmother became aware of what had happened. Mother would surely have been severely reprimanded if Gran had found out.

Finally the day arrived when the big farm wagon came for the apples. The cider would be made at the farm as Father did not have a cider press of his own.

The double gates were opened and the wagon slowly backed up our wide garden path, inching its way towards the house, the iron shoes of the horse making deep indentations in the hard packed earth. The chopping block and sawing horse were hastily pushed back out of the way and small sisters snatched up from under the wheels. Old Dobbin, my homemade rocking horse, with Mother's plait of hair for a tail and a knot in the wood for an eye, was also removed from its usual pasture alongside the path.

The apple heap had been bagged and these were soon loaded on the wagon and on their way to the farm, the cutter making quick work of turning the apples into small pieces, the green, red and yellow varieties all blending together as they were shovelled on to the bed of the cider press. Layer was placed upon layer, divided by clean, dry straw and then neatly squared off by a final clipping with straw shears. Weight and pressure was now applied to this cider cheese until the juice began to run in a steady trickle into the wooden vat below. More pressure would periodically be given and the huge beam of the press got lower and lower as the cider makers turned the cogs and wheels to apply more weight.

The oozings into the vat, too insipid as yet to be called cider, were a good thirst quencher and we knelt around the tub sucking the juice through straws which we gathered from the cider house floor.

Next evening, after tea, the iron wheels of the milk trucks could be heard rumbling up the road from the farm, carrying the first load of small barrels, full to overflowing with the sweet apple juice.

We ran to the gates to open them up for Father and to take the hurricane lantern from him and light his way up our uneven path.

The contents of the small barrels were soon transferred by wooden bucket and tun dish to the large barrels which by now were back in position in the outhouse. The bung at the top of the barrel was left out to allow for fermentation and in a few days the familiar 'wop wop' could be heard as the air found its way out. Our version of the childish game of not stepping on the lines of paving stones, was not to be caught in the outhouse when a barrel 'wopped': a difficult thing to avoid when several barrels were fermenting at the same time.

We, as children, considered the cider to be at its best after a few weeks, for it was then tangy and had developed a lovely sharp flavour which stung the mouth. Alas, this stage in its progress did not last very long, but we still continued to drink it.

The annual ritual of cidermaking may well have dominated the early autumn, but it was not the only annual task to be done.

The potatoes which Father planted in the plough ground, were dug, packed up and bagged. It was hard on the hands and made our skin dry, but we all helped out. None of us cared much for the work, but there was some compensation in the bumpy ride in the horse and cart across the fields to collect the bags.

For Gran autumn meant bonfires. Even in her old age she delighted in clearing her garden and orchard. The smoke could be seen for miles as it billowed its way up through the dying leaves of her walnut tree in the orchards.

One year, after a dry summer and autumn, Gran and Auntie who had been gardening and clearing up all day, decided to have a final go by setting fire to the dead grass at the bottom of the garden. Alas, this also set fire to the garden hedge and great panic ensued, everyone rushing around with buckets of water to douse the flames that leapt and crackled as they consumed the blackberry briars. It was a long way to the tap at the back of the house, but luckily Gran had several tin baths full of water on hand which she used for watering her plants, and the fire was soon put out.

In the afternoons the golden autumnal light burnished the landscape as the sun began to sink.

At night the stars seemed to shine with exceptional brilliance. Father took a great interest in astronomy. He pointed out the constellations to us and taught us how to find the Pole Star. One particular autumn the Aurora Borealis was exceptionally bright and we walked with Father to the railway bridge to get a better view of the glow in the northern sky. The bridge was the highest vantage point in an otherwise flat countryside and we had an uninterrupted view across to the Welsh hills and horizon. Father impressed on us that these Northern Lights were a natural phenomenon and not to be confused with the glow from the Welsh Steel Works which lit up the sky from time to time.

The Harvest and then the Hunter's moon rose full and bright in the east, silhouetting the big ash tree which grew in the field across the road. We ran to and fro, half mesmerised in the silver light, listening to the owls, imitating them and half scaring ourselves to death with talk of the ghosts and wolves who we imagined lurked behind every bush and corner.

Mother, who was afraid of nothing, would laugh as we rushed into the safety of the house and would remark that she had never met anyone worse than herself.

She had, as she said, 'Lived too long in the woods to be frightened by the owls!'

13
Christmas

The first frosts and winds of winter had cleared the trees of all remaining foliage. The yellowing leaves of the withies, flattened by sudden squalls, clung to the surface of the road like shoals of golden fish. Brown and yellow chrysanthemums were now the only spot of colour in the garden, and armfuls were cut and brought into the house. They glowed against the dark wainscot of the living room, their scent reaching everywhere. The winter song of robins, half heard, drifted sadly from quiet corners of the garden.

Mother, having studied the calendar, would announce that there would be a moon for Christmas. I never knew what this bearing had on the festivities, unless it was to light the way for Father Christmas on Christmas Eve.

We eagerly awaited the day Mother set aside each year for our Christmas shopping. Until then we secretly busied ourselves making as many presents as we could. Duchess sets were a great favourite to give to Gran or Auntie. We were taught to make these at school. When we first started embroidery classes, I thought, in my ignorance, that a Duchess set was some kind of fancy dress and was all for making one to add to our box of dressing up clothes.

We had all decided weeks in advance what we wanted for presents. Gran and Auntie gave us useful things such as underwear, face flannels and soap or nightdress cases. It was Mother we turned for the gifts we really wanted.

I had seen the very present I most wanted. It was an Actor's Outfit, beautifully laid out in a large eighteen by ten inch box. In it were all the greasepaints, powders, false hair pieces, moustaches and glue any producer of homemade entertainment could wish for. I had not realised such a thing could be bought and dreaded to think what it might cost. I had the sense to realise that it was probably more than Mother could afford to pay, and mentioned just casually what a wonderful present it would make.

A week before Christmas our money boxes were opened, and Father's pay cheque cashed in the village shop. Clutching our carefully written shopping lists, we ran alongside mother pushing the pram in a purposeful haste to town. As well as doing her general shopping the little extra money given to her by Father bought dates, figs, oranges and a box of cheap crackers.

Our goal, as always, was the Domestic Bazaar in Burnham High Street. This was the largest shop of its kind in town and at one time must have been a hall. Its counters displayed every kind of ware imaginable, stretching temptingly in rows the whole of its length to where a mural of a waterfall was painted on the end wall. Hidden music played on a theatre organ added still further to the glamour, and our excitement. We made our purchases with much deliberation and in great secrecy.

We then accompanied Mother to the grocers. Here there was the smell of smoked bacon, and sawdust on the floor. We loved to watch the money for the purchases and then the change fly forwards and backwards to the cash desk on overhead wires, and to hear the musical 'ping' as the container reached the end of its journey. The assistants were polite and kind to Mother, especially the man with the waxed moustache who worked the bacon slicer. In my eyes his manner transformed her from the plodding little woman with the pram to the equal of a queen.

Our last call was to the sweetshop to collect the box of crackers which had been put by for us, Mother paying a few pence a week against the purchase. Also, no trip to town was complete without sweets to eat on the way home. My favourite buy was a 'pennorth of bits'. This consisted of a three cornered bag, full to overflowing of the scrapings and leftovers in the sweet jars. Mints and acid drops, marsh mallows, pieces of rock, chocolates and liquorice allsorts, all mixed together in one glorious hotch potch of flavours and textures. It was by far the best buy for a penny.

Fighting usually broke out between us on the way home. My two younger sisters took more time over their sweets and upset them on the pram cover, whereupon they were chided by Mother for being so 'scammish' and further provoked by me as I darted in like a hovering hawk to sample their selection.

After tea had been cleared away we set to work to make up the packets of coloured gummed paper into paper chains to decorate the living room. These, threaded through the handles of the paper lanterns which we had been taught to make at school, made quite cheap Christmas decorations, although care had to be taken not to hang them to near the chimney of the oil lamp.

We had our own misletoe growing from a Sweet Blenheim tree in Gran's orchard. Grandfather had planted a berry in a crevice of the bark many years ago and this had now grown into a sizeable clump. Father brought home holly branches from the farm.

The sight and smell which epitomised Christmas was the Christmas tree. This was a branch cut from one of the large cypress trees which grew in abundane in the village. Potted in a large bucket it was placed in the corner of the room ready for decoration. Tinsel and other baubles carefully stored away from the previous Christmas were brought out and packets of sweets wrapped in silver paper were donated by Gran with strict instructions to put them on the tree and not to eat them before Chrismas Day.

One year, Auntie had brought home a net of chocolate coins wrapped in gold paper. These were placed on the tree and I watched over them for days, hardly able to await the cutting down and handing over for eating. Anticipation, however, soon turned into disappointment, for when opened the chocolate inside the foil was found to be mildewed and the only one to benefit was Lassie the dog. How her brown eyes brightened and her tail wagged as she was fed each coin.

Father's Christmas box from his employers was a piece of beef from one of the steers bred on the farm for the Christmas Fat Stock Show at Highbridge. This he brought home in triumph on Christmas Eve to join the chicken which had been killed, dressed and stuffed ready. Mother would be up very early on Christmas morning to light the oil stove in good time for the roasting. Oil stoves could be very temperamental if the wind was in the wrong direction and a draught came through the kitchen door.

We, too, would be awake long before the sound of church bells drifted across the fields from the neighbouring villages, or cockerels luckily enough to have escaped the Christmas slaughter, greeted the dawn.

Oh the joy of that Christmas morning when I realised that Mother had bought me the Actor's Outfit. She had kept it quiet, not only I suspect from me, but from Father and Gran as well. I never did find out how she managed to afford it. It was the most wonderful present I had ever received: now our Mexican characters could boast real drooping moustaches instead of those painted on with burnt cork.

It was customary to have tea with Gran on Christmas Day.

Her big kitchen table was pulled out from the wall and the best tablecloth laid over it. Her second best tea service was brought out from the front room sideboard. Tinned pears or peaches would be served and we were made to eat bread and butter with each helping. A fruit cake baked by Gran and covered with thick almond paste and icing, stood in the centre of the table on its glass cakestand. I could never get enough almond paste and hovered around in the hope that someone would say they did not want all theirs. Once we had eaten, we pulled crackers under the watchful eye of a bewhiskered Gladstone who stared sternly down from his gilt frame on the wall.

Then into Gran's front room where the round table with its chenille cloth was pushed aside to make more room. Here we played 'Gathering Nuts in May', Gran pretending she was not strong enough to pull us over to her side, while the leather bottoms of our new slippers slithered and slid on the thick coconut matting which covered the flagstoned floor. We sang songs, paper hats on head. Grandmother's favourite which she always sang at Christmas time was one which entreated its listeners to 'Never forget the dear ones that cluster round the home'. We all joined in the chorus of 'never forget, never forget' with great gusto.

Grandfather's accordian would be brought down from up-stairs where Gran had lovingly preserved it since his death. No one could play it, but Father did try, taking to the floor in a kind of shuffling dance which we clapped and applauded with vigour.

Mother retired early to our part of the house with my two younger sisters, who were now tired and crotchety and well past their bedtime. Jocelyn and I stayed behind in Gran's and played draughts, ludo or cards until we ourselves were sent home by Gran.

Mother, meanwhile, as a special Christmas treat had heated up a saucepan of cider to which she had added sugar and ginger. This made a delicious bedtime drink.

Drowsy and happy we made our way upstairs to where our younger sisters, Margaret and Pauline, were already sound asleep in what Mother always referred to as our 'trundle beds'.

14
Winter Days

The coldest and most dreary weather came after Christmas, and weekends excepted it seems I rarely saw home in daylight.

An oil lamp lit our breakfast table and I hated the moment when Mother turned down the wick and blew out the flame, plunging the room into near darkness. We knew it would be cold outside and the bleak prospect of the two mile journey to school on our bikes made us shudder.

Woollen gloves, palms uppermost, were laid on the fender to warm, and extra scarves were found to tie over our heads and ears. If the roads were icy we left home much earlier for we knew we would have to walk most of the way.

We sometimes met Father, struggling across the road to the home ground with a pitch of hay over his shoulder for the dry beasts. The animals, upon hearing the sound of his hobnailed boots ringing on the frosty road, clustered around the gate, their breath rising in clouds on the cold air. Father, his face partially obscured by the hay and the turned down brim of his trilby, looked blue and cold, and his nose, which could never be called straight, seemed more crooked than usual.

'Take care on the bridge', he would shout as we passed 'It's like glass up there'.

Half way to school we laid our bikes against the hedge and whacked our arms to bring life to our frozen fingers. By the time we had reached Burnham the feeling was just beginning to return to them and we felt sick with the pain.

If it was very wet, I was sent, in good time, to ask if I

might be allowed to ride to school with a friend who lived in a farm further up the village. They owned the first and only car we had seen. I hated asking for this favour, but Gran insisted. It embarrassed me to wait in the farm kitchen while they finished their breakfast porridge and was glad I did not have to ask for a lift too often.

But it was not the frost and rain which worried me. It was the high winds which blew with gale force intensity across the flat countryside, with nothing to break their progress between us and the Atlantic Ocean.

I recall once having to walk all the way home from school, in spite of its being a following wind, for fear of being blown into a ditch. Upon reaching the railway bridge, which did not have any sheltering hedges, I could make no progress at all. I tried to keep hold of my little bike and at the same time hang on to the railings, as the wind alternatively flattened and pulled me against them.

Mother was fighting to keep the pram from being tipped over and there was little she could do to help me. She eventually managed to grasp my coat and telling me to leave my bike by the roadside for Father to collect later, made me cling to the pram for the rest of the way home.

'I shall tell my grannie when I get home', I sobbingly repeated again and again, hardly knowing what I was saying because of the terror which gripped me.

We were met by Gran who was halfway down the garden path anxiously looking out for us. Seeing my tear-stained face, she whisked me away to where a dish of baked apples had just been taken out of the oven. With each mouthful, the terror began to subside I told her the story of the wind. Although still heaving the odd sob I soon felt better. Telling Gran was like telling God. Only she wielded more authority than he did.

A week of hard frost and cold easterly winds froze the ditches, rhines and ponds. We walked miles along the frozen watercourses, the ice snapping and cracking under our feet. The reeds on the railway pond were full of chattering starlings which flew up in their thousands as one black cloud when we approached. The ice on the smaller pond was firm enough to walk on and we were able to explore the little islands which had grown up in the middle of it and were out of reach the rest of the year.

A passing farmworker, worried by our boldness, remarked dourly, 'Best to come in off that, it bain't safe, and I doan't want to be in at the inquest when thees be brought out drowned'.

He needs not have worried. We had been brought up to look after ourselves and not to take unnecessary risks.

The cold winds continued to blow for weeks and the deeper pond also became frozen. Skaters from town came and showed off their skills by performing figures of eight on the ice. Forty boys from a private school arrived one afternoon with a master in charge and made long slides from bank to bank.

We ransacked a box of junk and found two pairs of ice skates which had been given to us years ago. We tied them to our shoes and tried to copy the style of the experienced skaters. Before the thaw had set in we were able to give a good imitation of the Skaters' Waltz with vocal accompaniment.

At home, the doors had wide gaps at the bottoms through which the draught blew most cruelly. Old coats laid down kept back most of this. In the real depth of winter the middle door in the passage was closed at night. It was usually kept open all the year round and propped back with a flatiron without a handle. Thus closing it was an extreme step, for it meant that light which normally showed from the two small glass panels of the front room door was cut off. Gran or Auntie, confidently striding along in the dark from their back door to ours, would enter the passage unable to see. Not having heard our shouted warnings until too late, they would suddenly crash into the closed middle door. Loud and long were the recriminations which followed.

One winter, when snow and wet had taken their toll on Father's boots, which in spite of regular dubbing had started to leak, he announced one evening that he intended taking the bus to Bridgwater to buy a new pair. Bridgwater was always considered the best place to purchase outdoor garments and foot wear for farmworkers.

This proposed trip was an unprecedented step for Father, but as the 'Johnny Fortnight' man no longer called because of ill health, Father was unable to buy or order his requirements at the door.

So dressed in his best and only suit, he set off early after breakfast. He was like a child on a Sunday School outing with Mother dancing attendance on his 'clobber', as he called it. Having recently spent a few days with Auntie at Lynmouth Foreland Lighthouse, I think he was beginning to get a liking for the big world outside the village.

Mother had drummed into him the times of the buses back and we eagerly awaited his return.

Anticipation, however, soon turned to horror when Mother was hastily summoned to the top of the village road. Here Father was stretched out on the grass verge, bleeding profusely from his nose and a cut on his forehead. The bus was there, pulled into one side, and from its driver Mother learnt that Father had tried to alight before the vehicle had stopped. He had fallen on his face.

The ambulance had been sent for and as it came clanging down the turnpike, Mother's heart was as lead. She was sure

Father was dying.

However, when cleaned up and three stitches put in his forehead, so dire a fate seemed less likely, but he was kept in hospital for two days.

The news of the accident soon spread around the village, and with it the inevitable rumours.

One of these was that Father had been drinking and had been tipsy when he fell off the bus. This we knew to be untrue. Father never went into pubs, he disliked beer and would certainly not drink pub cider.

Mother, now recovered from the terrible shock of seeing Father prostrate and bloodied at the roadside, took all the rumours calmly and dismissed the villagers remarks with a sniff.

'Some of 'em would say anything but their prayers', she retorted. 'And those they whistle'.

She made sure that Father was accompanied on all trips after that.

15

The End of Childhood

With my fourteenth birthday lying ahead, 1936 was to be a year of decision. What was I going to do when I left school? Some of my friends, my sister Jocelyn among them, had passed 'the scholarship'. They would be able to stay on at school until they were sixteen. How I envied them. Although as Mother said, and quite rightly, if I had taken the trouble to go to early morning classes as most of them had done, and put my mind to it, I could have been there as well.

Anyway, there was one consolation, I didn't have to wear those awful thick black stockings which were part of the uniform. From what Jocelyn told me it seemed to be all rules and regulations at Grammar School.

The country boys had jobs waiting for them on farms. Many of the town boys were already working evenings and weekends as errand boys for local shops and would be taken on full time when their schooling was finished. A few more ambitious, were hoping to become articled to accountants and solicitors. General shopwork and hairdressing were favourites for girls, and by the time most of them were fourteen they knew where they were to be employed.

With six months to go until my birthday I had made up my mind what I wanted to do. Arriving home from school one day I announced at tea-time that I was going to work in an office and had put my name down to start shorthand and typewriting classes two nights a week at the technical school in Burnham.

'Can you do it?', asked Mother, rather aghast at my boldness. 'What will Grannie say?'.

'Of course I can do it', I replied. 'And I neither know or care what Grannie will say. I am going to do something I want to do for a change'.

Gran had been saying for months past that the best employ-ment for a young girl was to go out into domestic service. I think she had visions of me living in at one of the big houses outside of town, answering the door in a cap and apron and learning all the domestic skills for when I had a home of my own. I must admit that my knowledge of these skills was quite negligible. I know Gran loved us dearly and wanted the best for us, but it was not quite what I had in mind for myself. I was rather fed up with being at the bottom of the social ladder and an office job would be a step upwards.

I was beginning to resent Gran's hold on the family, and had started to rebel.

We had been forced since early childhood to take purga-tives each week in the form of California Syrup of Figs, Senna Pods or Epsom Salts. Gran insisted they were necessary, but they were all equally horrible.

I loved figs. They grew over the orchard wall from next door and during the summer we stuffed ourselves with them. They ripened to the mauve and yellow colour of bruised flesh and had a wonderful taste. The bottled syrup we were forced to take by the spoonful bore no comparison and made me feel sick.

I had decided that enough was enough.

Having made up my mind about attending evening classes Mother thought I ought to have a new bike. The poor old milk bike was long past its prime. So my savings were drawn from the school savings bank and a new bike bought. It had to be a Raleigh, of course, for Auntie and Uncle had a few shares in the Raleigh Company.

Battery powered bicycle lamps had now taken the place of the old carbide lighting. My new lamp cast a pattern of light like aeroplane wings, the tips touching the hedges on either side of the road.

I was not frightened of the dark ride home after evening classes, but pedalled a little faster as I left the last street light behind me and was glad when I saw Father's burly figure and heard his familiar shout of 'Aye aye' challenging me from the darkness of the roadside. He would come part way on foot to meet me.

I knew it would not be easy to find an office juniors' job but I was quite prepared to wait. I had agreed that I would take any job that became available until such time as I found what I wanted. Indeed, Mother had heard of a hat shop which wanted a school leaver to help serve, so we went along for an interview.

It was a stuffy little shop, small and depressing and smelling of dusty carpets. Also I hated hats. The only hat I had ever wanted was one that had been given to Mother. It was the colour of Parma violets and made of thick shiny straw which crackled when touched. Gran said it was too old for me and would not let me wear it. I lost interest in hats after that.

I didn't care much for the proprietress of the shop either, but agreed to start work on the following Monday.

During the weekend I had second thoughts. I definitely did not want to sell hats. A postcard was sent informing the lady of my change of mind. Father decided I was very hard to please.

Then we heard that a lady who had taught me in infant shool wanted a young girl to help with the housework and take her small daughter for walks in the afternoons. I went along and renewed my acquaintance with her, and it was agreed that I start work immediately. I was to be paid nine shillings a week and my dinner would be provided. Mother made it quite clear that I was on the look out for an office job, and this was understood.

Although not fond of housework I dutifully carried out my chores of washing, carpet sweeping and dusting, and the morning soon passed. After the dinner dishes had been stacked away I set off with the small girl in the pushchair and a young pup on a leash, yapping at my heels.

Some days we walked into town and back, or did a circular trip around the big houses and tree lined road where their home was situated. More often we took the footpath across the sand dunes to the beach. Here the dog could be let free to scamper madly around the narrow paths between the sea buckthorn and spartina grass. I loved the mud flats, the sand dunes and the miles of clean, golden sand in between. They seemed to stretch for ever and brought verses of the 'Forsaken Merman' unbidden to my mind.

I was still attending evening classes and had made many new friends. Under the popping gas lights I began to master the rudiments of shorthand. Gramalogues and F and V hooks no longer held terrors for me and I found a typewriter much more to my liking than a sewing machine.

Knowing I was on the lookout for an office job, one of my new friends told me of a vacancy in her office for a junior clerk. She had already mentioned my name to the head clerk and I was asked along for an interview. When I announced my news at home that evening, Father immediately dampened my enthusiasm.

'You can't leave that poor woman in the lurch', said he, referring to my employer. 'Surely you've got eyes'.

'Of course I've got eyes', I smartly replied, 'She knows I am looking for an office job. If I don't get one soon I shall be too old to get in as a junior'.

Father was referring to the fact that the lady was expecting her second child within a few weeks, a fact which had never been discussed with me.

I had to ask my employer for a reference to take to the interview. She was a little upset at first but finally agreed. I proudly bore off a note describing me as her 'general factotum in the home'. I thought it sounded grand, whatever it might mean.

Backed up with a word from my headmaster I got the job and was to start on April 1st. Mother said April Fool's Day was a bad choice for embarking on a new job. My starting wage was to be £13 a calendar month and I was required to sign a form in which I promised to keep inviolate all affairs of the Company. It was all very important.

I was now on my way to my fifteenth birthday and still wore my hair in two long plaits.

'Do you think', my new employer asked, slightly embarrassed, 'You could wear your hair up?' In his opinion plaits were out of place in a business office. A school friend who had taken up hairdressing was the one to wield the scissors.

With money of my own I was now able to spend holidays more frequently with my aunt and uncle. In 1939 they were living at Lynmouth Foreland lighthouse in North Devon. I had arranged to spend my week's holiday with them and set off, on my own, by train from Highbridge to Minehead, and then by coach for the remainder of the journey.

It was the day after Neville Chamberlain had returned from Munich waving the piece of paper which he said, and everyone hoped, meant peace in our time. Father had been saying for a long while there was going to be another war soon.

As I watched the Devon countryside rolling by I felt very grown up and happy. Here was I, off travelling on my own for a holiday and the impending war had been averted. All was right with my world.

But not so far away in Europe all was not right.

On the 3rd September 1939 the Second World War was declared. Father had been right again.

That Sunday evening, as the September dusk closed around the familiar landscape, Father suggested a walk to the railway bridge. Everything looked the same. A group of cows chewed contently by the gate of the milking field. The row of chestnut trees in the copse dropped ripe conkers as we passed. Squashed prickly casings littered the lane where children from town had been gathering them during the day. The rookery elms, untouched as yet by autumn, stood tall and serene as they always had done, their noisy summer occupants fledged and flown.

Two swans, glowing white against the deep, black water of the pond, rested motionless in the silence.

We reached the railway bridge and looked around us.

We had come on this occasion not to see lights in the sky, but to ponder on their absence. Not a glimmer could be seen from the town or surrounding countryide. All was dark. The blackout had begun.

I understood more clearly now why Grandmother had been so anxious to find the old green roller blind for her kitchen window. She had packed it in a trunk in 1918.

I notice that the windows of My Lady's manor house, which usually shone out like beacons from their elevated position, were now dark and cheerless. The garish lighting from the Fox and Goose inn on the turnpike road, always a landmark at night, no longer lit up the sky..

The lights had gone out again all over Europe.

Standing in silence, Father and I stared into the dusk, each busy with our own thoughts.

I was thinking of Gran and that other war of not so very long ago when she had stood alone in her anguish on this same bridge.

For the first time in my life I felt very close to Father. I wanted to thank him but the words would not come. I knew with a sudden grown-up awarness that our lives would never be quite the same again, that the carefree days of my childhood had come to an end.

We stayed for a while, close but unable to communicate, unwilling to relinquish our hold and hasten the end of something which was already slipping away from us.

Then, with thoughts and words unspoken, we retraced our steps to home.